THE MiDDLE SCHOOL SURViVAL GUiDE

THE MiDDLE SCHOOL SURViVAL GUiDE

ARLENE ERLBACH

ILLUSTRATIONS BY HELEN FLOOK

WALKER & COMPANY

NEW YORK

First published in the United States of America in 2003 by
Walker Publishing Company, Inc.

Published simultaneously in Canada by
Fitzhenry and Whiteside, Markham, Ontario L3R 4T8

For information about permission to reproduce selections from this book, write to
Permissions, Walker & Company, 104 Fifth Avenue, New York, New York 10011

Library of Congress Cataloging-in-Publication Data

Erlbach, Arlene.
The middle school survival guide / Arlene Erlbach ; illustrations by Helen Flook.
p. cm.
Includes index.
Summary: A guidebook to help deal with changes in school, families,
social lives, and bodies that come during the middle school years,
with specific advice for a variety of situations.
Contents: A new school, a new environment—Teachers—Academics—Peers—
The opposite sex—Home life—Puberty—Really serious stuff—Being yourself.

ISBN 0-8027-8852-1—ISBN 0-8027-7657-4 (paperback)

1. Middle school students—Life skills guides—Juvenile literature.
2. Preteens—Life skills guides—Juvenile literature. 3. Teenagers—Life skills
guides—Juvenile literature. 4. Adolescent psychology—Juvenile literature.
[1. Life skills. 2. Middle schools. 3. Schools.] I. Flook, Helen, ill. II. Title.
LB1135 .E75 2003
373.18—dc21
2002034784

The illustrations for this book were created using FW artist's acrylic inks on a smooth-surface
Fabriano 50 percent cotton watercolor paper.

Book design by Chris Welch

Visit Walker & Company's Web site at www.walkerbooks.com

Printed in the United States of America

4 6 8 10 9 7 5 3

To Elyse O'Connor, who gave me the idea; Herb and Matt Erlbach, for their support; and Paul Robinson, for believing in Matt. —A. E.

To Macsen (my son), who survived middle school and lived to tell the tale, and to Roland, for always believing in me. —H. F.

Special thanks to the following people for their incredible help: Heidi Bartelsein and the kids at Parkview School; Dana Kanwischer and her students at Niles West High School; Pat Harn-Moir; Patricia Harris; Sue Currie; Madeline Fuerstch; Dr. Susan Mackey; Katie Naka; Chris Naka; Mallory Portnoy; Abby Winograd; Kai Peterson; and Stina Peterson. —A. E.

CONTENTS

iNTRODUCTiON

Am I There Yet, or What?

It can be the best of times. It can be the worst of times, too. This book is about the stuff that happens when you're in middle school or junior high—the place where you go after life in elementary school ends and before high school begins. Middle school happens at that weird time in life when you're not a teenager and not a little kid. Middle school means being a middle-aged kid.

In middle school you'll deal with teachers who expect more work than before, with competitive cliques, and with taking it all off in front of strangers during gym. Middle school also involves lots of issues that happen outside school, like relating to friends and family on a different level,

1

and parties where kids want to kiss and do more. So even though this book is called *The Middle School Survival Guide*, it includes information about how to deal with other concerns.

Middle school kids were even asked about what really bugs them, and you'll be able to read their responses and advice. For certain scenarios, they revealed suggestions about how to deal with common middle school annoyances as well as major hassles. So, for some situations, you'll find out what other kids have actually done to solve problems. You'll be assured that you're not the only kid on the planet who has experienced middle school ups and downs.

WHAT IS MIDDLE SCHOOL, ANYWAY?

Even if you're living under a rock, you'll probably know exactly when you're in middle school. At the end of fourth, fifth, or sixth grade, your current school holds a big-deal graduation at which you're strongly warned to behave like ladies and gentlemen, then given a pat on the back. The graduation happens because you've completed your education at one place. Now you're going up to another level.

The next year, you enter a place called So and So Middle School. No smiling apples or talking squirrels decorate the bulletin boards. A crossing guard doesn't stand at the corner to make sure you don't get hit by cars.

You've been used to staying in one room for most of the day. Now you have to travel through long hallways and up and down stairways to find your different classrooms, the bathroom, and the cafeteria. You and your classmates are the youngest. You don't rule anymore.

Not every town calls middle school middle school. Some places refer to it as junior high or upper school. If you go to a kindergarten-through-eighth-grade school, middle school still happens. Sometime between fifth and seventh grade, the picture changes drastically. You switch rooms for classes. You may even use a separate wing of the school. You're known as "the big kids." The little kids look up to you, and this might give you kind of a thrill.

In this book, you'll discover

- Why teachers give so much homework. There's a method to this madness. You'll find tips on how to get it done.
- How to deal with snoopy parents—and siblings.
- What really happens in the A clique. It's not as great as you think. Swear!
- Why parents treat you like a grown-up one minute and a baby the next.
- How to deal with gym showers.
- And lots more.

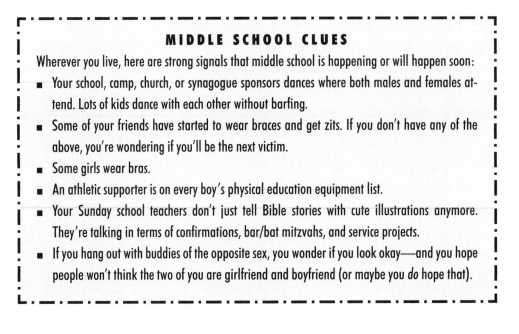

MIDDLE SCHOOL CLUES

Wherever you live, here are strong signals that middle school is happening or will happen soon:

- Your school, camp, church, or synagogue sponsors dances where both males and females attend. Lots of kids dance with each other without barfing.
- Some of your friends have started to wear braces and get zits. If you don't have any of the above, you're wondering if you'll be the next victim.
- Some girls wear bras.
- An athletic supporter is on every boy's physical education equipment list.
- Your Sunday school teachers don't just tell Bible stories with cute illustrations anymore. They're talking in terms of confirmations, bar/bat mitzvahs, and service projects.
- If you hang out with buddies of the opposite sex, you wonder if you look okay—and you hope people won't think the two of you are girlfriend and boyfriend (or maybe you *do* hope that).

You'll find out that middle school can be an awesome place with lots of challenges and new experiences. You'll be glad to know it's a place you can definitely handle without getting stressed out.

1
A NEW SCHOOL, A NEW ENVIRONMENT

Nobody asked me if I wanted to change schools.

To many kids, middle school means a new building that can be incredibly awesome, totally annoying, or just plain scary.

If your family has moved around regularly, maybe you're already used to the challenge of navigating your way around a new school, checking out people to eat lunch with, and figuring out what makes teachers tick. But to most kids, tackling the new-school scenario can be a major-league pain.

In this chapter you'll discover how

to work out problems that could happen simply because you're at an unfamiliar location.

School isn't only a place where you learn. It contains hundreds of bodies vying for popularity, a place on the team, and decent grades. Nobody wants to look too obvious about what his or her agenda includes. That's why it can become stress city.

GETTING LOST

Last year you could walk through the school blindfolded. You knew where everything was, from the janitor's office to the teachers' lounge. (In case you're wondering what really goes on there, the faculty hide in the lounge to eat lunch, de-stress, and gossip about students—just like you gossip about them.)

Your new school seems so humongous, with all its wings and floors; you wonder if you'll ever find out where you're going. You have nightmares about winding up in math class when you're supposed to be in social studies. You're terrified that you won't be able to find the bathroom when you need it fast!

The best way to deal with this is to call

the school over the summer and ask for a tour to check things out. If you feel weird about doing this, have one of your folks make the arrangements. Maybe you and a few buddies can go together. If one of you has an older sibling or friend who has gone to this place, bribe them to come along. They will be useful in letting you in on important information, such as which teachers are cool, which ones secretly hate kids, and if the mystery-meat casserole in the cafeteria really contains warmed-up cat food.

My brother let me shadow him one day when I was in sixth grade at his junior high. I didn't remember everything, but I felt a little better about going to the new school. And he and his friends told me who all the nice and rotten teachers were. —Arnold, age 12

After you find out the school's setup, do the following:

- Write down how the rooms are numbered. Numbering systems for classrooms are not always logical. Nobody has yet figured out if this is part of some deliberate scheme to make things difficult.
- Make sure you know important locations like the bathrooms, the cafeteria, and the gym.
- If you go to a school that sends out schedules in advance, go over them well. If possible, visit the school before it opens to make a dry run before that big first day.

If you follow these suggestions, you'll feel a lot better about the first few days of school.

LUNCHTIME TRAUMAS

Maybe you'll be *exceptionally* lucky. The friends you chowed down with in elementary school, or at least one of them, will have lunch the same period as you do, so you won't be chewing on your tuna sandwich and cheese curls alone. Or maybe everyone you know has lunch at another time or in a separate lunchroom. You imagine yourself eating alone for the entire year while everyone else is munching lunch with their best buddies and talking about what a dork you are. Here are some strategies to avoid lunchtime alone in Rejectland:

- If you know beforehand that you'll have no friends from your old school to eat lunch with, recruit lunch buddies ASAP. Think about kids you know from places like Scouts, the pool, camp, or your place of worship. Get on the phone and say hello.

■ *Case out the cafeteria during lunch. You may see somebody or several familiar warm bodies sitting at a table with an empty seat. These could be kids from your old school or from your soccer team, church, synagogue, or the camp you attend. It's hard, and this takes guts, but just ask if you can sit with them. —Gina, age 13*

EXTREME LUNCHTIME MEASURES

If you don't find somebody you know to eat with, here are a few more extreme methods for finding lunch buddies. Two of these approaches take guts, and a deep breath, but they will more than likely work:

■ *Search the cafeteria for a table with empty seats where kids appear to be friendly, and on your coolness level. Be very realistic in your assessment. Introduce yourself. Say, "Can I park myself here?" Unless these people are total jerks (then you don't need these kids for friends), they'll allow you to sit there and may become your regular lunch crowd. —Meghan, age 14*

- *Sit down alone with homework, or an exciting and popular magazine or book. Pretend you're above the noontime scene, even though you aren't. —Annie, age 16*

Eating alone once in a while isn't the end of the world. You might decide to do lunch solo one day, and a person you don't know might plop themselves down at your table and become a friend.

LOCKER COMBO AMNESIA

Some of us are great at learning anything having to do with numbers. Just give one of these people a series of numerals to remember, and she'll run them off as though she has a computer in her head. Most people's minds don't operate like that, so locker combinations are hard to remember—at first. Here's how to remember yours:

- Write it down. Put it on a little card. Repeat it over and over again until you remember it.

  - *Type the numbers on your computer—print it out, but don't put your name on it. That way nobody will know whose it is if you lose it. —Jason, age 12*

- Stick it in your purse, bookbag, or wallet, where it won't get lost. Remember not to include your name, locker number, or doodling that can be identified as yours. After you dial the numbers for a week or so, they'll become second nature, like your best friend's phone number. Just in case you have one of those days when you'd forget your head if it weren't attached, leave the number in your wallet at all times.

Make sure you have a copy of the locker combination in a safe place at home. That way you'll have a copy of it if it falls out of your wallet. If you ever do think somebody may have gotten hold of it, talk to your school office ASAP and get the combination changed. In some cases you may need to purchase a new lock.

SIBLING IMPRESSIONS

If you're the first in your family to attend your school, the principal, teachers, and rest of the staff probably won't have any preconceived notion about you, unless you show up with an earring in your nose, blue hair, and jeans full of holes. But if you had a brother or sister whom teachers remember fondly, or whom the faculty couldn't stomach, some of the staff may expect you to behave just like the genius, or troublemaker, who came before you. What follows is a sampling of typical sibling impressions, how they might affect your teachers' expectations of you, and what to do to combat them.

The Einstein Clone

The first day, you might be greeted with, "I just loved having Ashley [or Albert] in my class." Any teacher would. An A minus was a low grade for this sibling. You know that this won't happen with you unless you have a complete brain restructuring. Your talents lie elsewhere. That's cool.

Not everybody has the brain cells, discipline, or motivation to be an incredible student. Most kids and adults are really good at one or a few things, and average or not so terrific at others. It's true that a few kids exist who excel at everything. They get

A's in all their academic subjects, and in art, music, and gym, too. They'd probably ace lunch if teachers graded it! If your brother or sister blew the grading curve off the school's tests, and you won't be repeating the performance, here's what to do:

- *Everyone knows who my brother is because he's a real brain. So I was afraid to start a new school because he's, like, so smart. But the teachers never said anything to me except "I enjoyed having your brother." I do my work and get Cs and Bs, and nobody says anything to me about not being as smart. —Edgar, age 12*

- If a teacher repeatedly compares you to a past sibling, explain that the two of you are separate entities, and that's how you'd like to be treated. Unless, of course, you don't mind being compared to your sibling.
- Do your best. Even if you can't manage A or B work, turn in everything on time and neatly. Don't do annoying things like talking or passing notes in class. Your teachers will realize you aren't a carbon copy of your sibling, but they will appreciate that you're a nice kid.
- Join clubs or participate in extracurricular activities that will show off your talents and skills.
- Assess your strong points. Maybe you're very creative or a great friend. These traits are very important. Not everyone who was a stellar student has tremendous success in adulthood. And that's the absolute truth!

The Super Jock

If you have a sibling who was a sports star, this will definitely be remembered, too. That's great if you're sure you'll follow in his or her footsteps. But if balls and baskets make you barf, you may feel high-end humiliation when the phys ed teacher walks up to you and says things like, "I can't wait for you to try out for the team," or "See you at cheerleading auditions." You'll probably feel like crawling into the nearest hole and remaining there until middle school ends.

It's true that star athletes gain lots of respect, especially if they excel in football or basketball, or do cartwheels well enough to cheer the team on. But other people with talents rule, too. Develop your skills and explore your interests. The more you accept your own good points and appreciate them, the more other people will as well.

My cousin is the cheerleading captain. So my cousin, aunt, mother, and teachers thought

I'd try out. I really didn't want to. My mother kept telling me how cute I'd look in the uniform. Well, I did try out and didn't get in because I'm not good at cheerleading stuff. I joined the choir and newspaper. —Jessica, age 14

The Troublemaker

Maybe your brother was a classic juvenile delinquent. He earned detentions regularly for major infractions like smoking in the bathroom, disrupting classes, or starting food fights in the cafeteria. You know that when he went up to the next grade (or maybe he didn't, or he got expelled), the teachers celebrated. You may be an unpleasant reminder. Some teachers might shudder when they find out you're in their class, cringing and complaining, "Another monster from that family has landed." This might be part of the gossip in the teachers' lounge. But you're not like that at all. Sometimes you ask yourself if you or your brother might have been switched at birth. Here's how to knock your teachers' socks off and surprise the school staff:

- Always do what your teachers expect— and maybe a little more, too.
- Be on your best behavior, no matter what!

- Avoid friends who do things that earn detentions or suspensions.
- Participate in an extracurricular activity in which you're helping people, or one that troublemakers steer clear of.

Soon you'll be treated as an individual member of your family, not the clone of the evil sibling that previously darkened the school's hallways. Your teachers may *also* wonder if there was a mix-up in the hospital.

I have a sister who had a horrible reputation for cutting school, and she got suspended for smoking. I just acted like I always do—kind of quiet—and the teachers treated me like an okay kid. —Allen, age 13

BEING THE BABIES AT SCHOOL

Last year you and the kids in your class were considered hot stuff. Your class ruled. Most of the younger kids thought you were pretty awesome and respected you. Now you're in middle school. Your class doesn't run the school anymore.

Life goes in cycles. Sometimes you and your friends are on top. Then, because of circumstances beyond your control, another group takes over. Within a few months you'll get used to being a lowly fifth-, sixth-, or seventh-grader. Next year, or a few years from now, you'll be at the top end of the school again. Then right after you get your turn at the top again, you'll start high school, where the cycle repeats itself. The same thing happens after high school—when you go to college, vocational school, or take a job.

You'll find yourself starting at a new place where some people have been there longer and seem to know everything. That's okay. Soon you'll know as much as they do.

I felt kind of weird about not being the top group that had lots of attention and privileges when I started junior high. But I got used to it. The older kids were cool, and I made friends with two guys that were in seventh grade in the class ahead because we took orchestra together. They needed a bass player for their band and asked me to be in a special quartet. We're good friends. —Matt, age 13

2

TEACHERS

Are they really out to get me?

The good news about middle school is that you aren't stuck with one teacher all day. When you were in elementary school, you usually had one teacher for everything except special subjects like phys ed and art, or maybe for science or math. If you liked your teacher, school seemed like a tolerable place to spend six hours. If you hated your teacher, you couldn't wait until the last bell rang.

The bad news is that now you have lots of adult personalities to deal with. But that doesn't have to be an ordeal. In this chapter you'll discover how teachers tick.

THE CLASS OF ETERNAL TORMENT

For forty minutes or so every day you have a class that you wish were canceled forever. You cringe when the starting bell rings. You'll be glad when the school year is over so you won't have to spend another minute in that academic Dreadland again. Here are some tips to make an unpleasant class period more bearable:

- Think about what bothers you the most about the class—the teacher, the subject matter, or all of it combined.
- If the teacher seems not to like you, ask yourself some of these questions: Do I turn in sloppy work or forget homework? Do I stroll in after the bell or chat with friends during class? If any of these scenarios is the case, make this type of behavior history.
- Now maybe the teacher does seem hostile toward you. He or she gives you unreasonably low grades. You are subjected to such humiliation techniques as being picked on or yelled at in class. You may want your parents, or you and your parents, to have a confer-

ence with the teacher to straighten things out. Or maybe you want to hash it out with the school counselor first. Nobody has the right to make you feel like pond scum.

- If your brain cells just don't match up with the subject matter, you might need extra input, like hiring a tutor, asking a buddy for help, or even asking the teacher for extra help. Don't be embarrassed. Plenty of kids need outside assistance in certain subjects, even though they don't announce it.
- If the class is just plain boring, focus on doing your best. That way you won't find yourself repeating it in summer school.
- Maybe you're in the wrong level of the class, and you need to go higher or lower. Discuss this with your parents, the teacher, or your school counselor.

  - *If a teacher really has it in for you, tell your counselor. He or she may know about how the teacher operates and give you some clues on dealing with this person better. —John, age 12*

  - *Think about if the teacher is mean to everyone sometimes, not just you. Sometimes teachers do lots of yelling, and that's how they are. —Steve, age 12*

It's okay not to like all your teachers. But if you can't stand any of them (and this sometimes happens), you may want to ask yourself why, then discuss it with your school counselor.

WHAT TEACHERS EXPECT FROM KIDS

Teachers do not expect you to waltz into class daily with a smile pasted to your face and say, "Good morning, Mr., Ms., or Mrs. Educator, I'm dying to be here even though there's a blizzard outside, the bus broke down, and I had to walk six blocks without gloves." They don't for one second think you're going to turn in perfect home-work every time—or always do A+ work. Here is what teachers *would* love for you to do:

- Turn in work that's legible. Even if you have every answer correct, the teacher has lots of papers to grade. She doesn't want to spend extra time deciphering each answer.
- Put your name on every paper. Teachers don't want to play guessing games about whose work the nameless paper belongs to. In some cases, teachers trash these papers and count them as F's.
- Turn in your work on time. If you can't because your gold-

fish died, your long-lost uncle turned up for dinner, or you had a blowup with a friend, tell your teacher. Make arrangements to get it done as soon as possible—but don't make a habit of this.

- Ask for extra help when you don't understand something. The teacher won't think you're an idiot. It's his job to help you. He wants you to succeed.
- Don't whisper, write notes, or pass smoke signals in class.
- Always come prepared for class.
- Bring everything you need each day, like pencils, notebooks, pens, calculators, a magnifying glass, your completed homework, and anything else that is due.
- Raise your hand to speak.
  - *Teachers don't like you to shout out answers, even if you're dying to answer. —Mallory, age 14*
  - *Don't hand in messy papers or stuff that's all crumply. —Matt, age 14*

HOW TO CHARM TEACHERS

To wow a teacher and get one to *really* like you, do everything suggested in the previous section, and a bit more. Here are some of the extra things that make teachers tell other faculty members how wonderful you are during their lunchtime gossip sessions. These tactics may pay off if your grade is in between, and the teacher needs to make that big decision about giving you the higher or lower grade.

- Always say a pleasant hello.
- If a teacher presents an opportunity for extra credit, go for it.
- If a teacher has been really helpful, send a note saying how much you appreciate it.
- Offer to stay after school to help clean blackboards, shelve books, or help straighten up the room, if you have time.
- If you discover that your teacher likes iguanas, dogs, marigolds, or lamb chops, start a conversation about the subject. But not during class time. You'll get known as a brownnoser.
- Teachers and students alike can't stand tattletales. Don't rat on people unless they're doing something harmful like poking each other with scissors or attempting to light a fire in class.

- *Always act interested even if the class is real boring. —Showba, age 14*
- *Don't make jokes and laugh at people during class. —Chris, age 11*

Teachers are human. In most cases their intention is not to torture you. They usually became teachers because they like kids and want to help them learn.

3

ACADEMiCS

What do you mean, "It's why you're here in the first place"?

You may complain about getting up and going to school every morning. But be honest—in some ways it's really fun. You see your friends. You find out what everyone is wearing. You catch up on juicy gossip. It's the place where lots of exciting stuff, like an occasional food fight in the cafeteria or lovers'  quarrels, goes on. The main reason for school is not the social scene, though. It's about grades, acquiring life skills, and bringing home report cards that please you—and make your parents proud enough to make multiple copies and send them to friends and relatives out of town. In this chapter you'll discover how to deal with issues of academic success.

WHY DO TEACHERS GIVE SO MUCH HOMEWORK?

In elementary school, you probably thought teachers generally assigned a reasonable amount of homework. You could usually finish it in one night—or if an assignment was really long, the teacher usually gave you enough time to finish it without causing a panic attack.

Now you have four or five teachers. Sometimes you wonder if the principal is holding a competition, with a prize to the teacher who dishes out the most homework. That's *probably* not the case. Teachers give out homework for various reasons, none of which is to make your life miserable:

- They may want you to prepare for tomorrow's lesson, so that when they attempt a discussion about chapters 1 to 3 of *Sounder* in English or reading class, you won't think that the main character is a kid that likes to make all kinds of noises.

- They want you to go over what you learned that day to make sure it sticks to your brain cells.
- Sometimes what they need to teach you takes a long time to learn. Part of the learning needs to be done at home or the topic will take up all year.
- Some school districts require teachers to give a certain amount of homework each night. These rules may be so clear they are written in the school district's rule book for teachers. Principals even check up on teachers, to make sure they pile on the expected amount of homework.

You can't stop teachers from giving out homework—even if you start an antihomework revolution. So here are some ways to deal with it:

- Finish it right after school. This way, you can have the rest of the day to veg out in front of the tube, e-mail, talk on the phone, shoot baskets, train your parrot to speak Latin or Swahili, or hang out with your friends.
- Take a break after school. Finish it after dinner, when your brain is clearer.
- Break up assignments. Do some homework, play with the dog. Do some homework, then do something else that's fun. Then go back to homework.
- Turn homework into a group activity. Do it with a friend or sibling. At least you won't feel so alone—and there is someone to gripe with.

  - *Take your favorite snacks to the place where you do your homework. —Brianna, age 11*

The most important thing about homework is to get it done. Even if you aren't a top student, if you make the effort to hand in homework on time, you'll please the teacher. He will know you're actually making an effort.

THE ASSIGNMENT FROM THE BLACK LAGOON

Sometimes a teacher gives out an assignment that seems impossible. It's long. You can't understand it. It involves lots of research and written work, or math knowledge that only rocket scientists possess. You're terrified you'll get a horrendous grade on it—or never finish it. You have anxiety attacks whenever you think about it.

When this happens, calm down. Look over the assignment. Think about what's freaking you out. Then use some of these tactics:

- Make an appointment to see the teacher. Tell her what's bugging you. She will probably go over it with you.

- *Ask another adult or older sibling to explain the assignment to you and give you tips about dealing with it. —Rabia, age 12*

- If the assignment will take days or weeks to complete, do it little by little. Don't try to wrap it up in one evening while you're sitting in front of the tube. Make a schedule of when you expect to complete each portion of the assignment. Make sure you allow extra time in case your cat throws up on it, or the books you need at the library aren't available.

  - *See if you can talk to somebody a year ahead of you who has had that teacher or class. Maybe they'll give you the info you need on how to get it done. —Luis, age 11*

CAN PARENTS HELP?

Of course your folks can help you with an assignment. But doing your work for you is not part of the parent–kid contract. You're the one who'll be receiving the grade, not them. Ditto for older brothers, sisters, friends, grandparents, aunts, uncles, or cousins. They were in middle school already and don't have to give a repeat performance. Here's what counts as fair assistance on schoolwork from parents or anyone else:

- Advising how to edit a paper, not doing the paper for you.
- Providing alternate examples of how to work out a problem correctly.
- Going over an assignment and telling you what is incorrect, but not actually correcting it.
- Giving you strategies on how to approach an assignment.

- Demonstrating how to set up a major project, such as how to use the video camera or other equipment you need for an assignment.
- Helping you create outlines for illustrations on a project that you don't quite have the skill to do.
- Showing you where in the library you might find useful information.
- Purchasing or suggesting supplies that would make your project more attractive.
- Helping you navigate the Internet.

GROUP PROJECTS

In middle school, teachers may assign group projects. A group project can be fun, or a disaster. Sometimes the teacher decides who's in each group. This guarantees complaints, because kids might be selected to work with people they wouldn't consider getting near.

Sometimes you may be able to choose your own group. This doesn't mean you should recruit your best buddies and make the project into a party. Group projects have been known to cause squabbles among friends, or even

end friendships, because certain group members didn't pull their weight. It's not easy to tell your best friend that she is being a total goof-off—and then threaten to inform the teacher about her laziness.

Group projects work best when people doing the project together have different skills, like a great artist, a computer whiz, a writer, and a researcher. Here are some hints to make your group project not give you nightmares:

- Before you begin, have everyone discuss what their strengths and weaknesses are. This way the group can decide on each person's responsibility.

  - *Decide who's going to be in charge. Then have each person discuss what they're going to do. The person in charge should check up on everyone without being a pain or too bossy. —Sarah, age 13*

- Set a date when each part of the project needs to be completed. Meet every few days. Discuss where everyone is on their part of the work.
- Finish a few days beforehand so that you can correct any problems. This way, if somebody's dog really chewed up the project or drooled on it, you have time for damage control. These things can really happen.
- If somebody isn't doing his fair share, see what you can do to resolve the problem. Have the group members speak up about their concerns. Give the person at fault an opportunity to discuss why he isn't pulling his weight. If things don't change, warn him that you'll inform the adult in charge. This isn't tattling. It's taking care of yourself.

■ *Work with people who you know will do decent work—not kids you want to get to know better, because you think that they're cool. —Meg, age 12*

BRAIN-POOL LABELS

By middle school you probably have an idea of where you stand in the brain pool. Being in the middle usually feels okay. That's where most kids, adults, dogs, elephants, and other creatures would rate. But it's often hard to handle the label of genius or dummy.

Feeling Dumb

Does everyone do better than you in school? Do you have to work extra hard to maintain Cs? Do you often receive Ds and Fs, no matter what you do? This feels awful. You wonder if when brains were handed out, you received the one with missing parts. Not doing well at a place where you spend a good part of the day feels horrendous, for sure. Here are tactics for dealing with the situation:

■ Ask a trustworthy friend for help. You don't need to say, "I'm between a D or an F in everything, and I might get held back a year." Just ask for some tips on how to do better. If the friend is a true friend, he will be glad to show you how to improve without blabbing.

Do you feel dumb because you go to the type of school where only A students are considered human? Some schools operate like that. Most of the world is not made up of A students. Not all report-card stars are megasuccesses later in life, either. You're probably good at something that doesn't involve outstanding academic skills. Good for you!

■ Consider activities that happen outside school, like at the YMCA or other community centers. You'll discover some talents. You may meet new friends who have no idea about your school performance.
■ Join activities that focus on what you're good at, or what you like to do.
■ Maybe you need to have your course load adjusted or to take courses on a different level. This does not mean you're defective goods. It just means that at this place and time in your life, you need extra help.
■ Maybe you need to be tested for an undiagnosed learning disability. It's not the end of the world. Plenty of successful and creative people have learned to adapt to learning disabilities. Ax the word *disability* from the label. Think of it as a difference in learning styles.

I have a learning disability. It's not such a big deal. I see a special teacher for reading and she shows me how to read better. She helps me read the hard words for the story problems in math. It's in another room at my school. There's a couple other kids who are in this group with me, and we work together to learn. The teacher is pretty nice and jokes around. So it's not too bad to go there. —Jessica, age 11

■ If you are having serious trouble keeping up with schoolwork, talk to your counselor, parents, or teachers.

FEELING TOO SMART

Maybe you're one of those kids who find school easy. You get As in everything. You finish your homework with time to spare. This could make other kids envious. Your status also may encourage teasing about being a nerd or geek. Usually this happens because kids are jealous—or maybe grades don't mean much to them. That's their choice. Here are some tips to handle this dilemma so that you won't be treated badly.

■ Be modest.
■ Don't make regular announcements about how wonderful your grades are. Keep your test grades and report card grades to yourself. If people ask, just say it's personal.
■ If teachers like reporting who blew the curve off a test—or what a wonderful essay you did—tell them you appreciate the praise, but you'd like to keep it private.

- You may want to think about being considered for higher-level courses or a gifted-students program, if your school district offers those options. Maybe a community college or high school will allow you to take courses or lend you some of their textbooks in the subjects that interest you.

- Help kids who aren't doing as well in school as you are. Being smart is a gift like any other. Make the best of it without making other people think you're better than they are.

I'm good at math, so I help other people with their math problems, if they need it. —Vance, age 13

I try to keep my grades to myself, so people won't hang out with me or not hang out with me for being smart. —Steve, age 13

Cheating

Cheating happens anytime that you get credit for work you didn't do, by being dishonest, sneaky, and deceptive. You also cheat when you help someone else cheat. When you're stressed out, devious methods of receiving a better grade may go through your head. And it's tempting to help a friend cheat when she becomes unglued about an assignment or test. Cheating can cause serious trouble; your parents might be called, or you might be suspended. In some situations, you might be expelled. Not to mention that it can leave a permanent mark on your academic record. Cheating isn't worth it. In case you weren't sure, here are some examples of cheating:

- Hiding answers to a test in your wallet, bookbag, or purse.
- Peeking at somebody else's paper, or allowing someone to take a look at yours, during the test.
- Having somebody write a paper for you or writing one for somebody else. Common variations of this are recycling somebody else's paper and saying it's yours or purchasing a paper from any person or organization that sells ready-made papers.
- Asking somebody questions during a test.
- Receiving an unauthorized copy of a test and using it to study from.

Getting together with friends to do homework and compare answers does not qualify as cheating. It doesn't mean that outside of class you can't have

somebody look over an assignment to show you how to improve it. And if your teacher allows it, your friends can help you during class.

OTHER ACTIVITIES THAT COUNT AS CHEATING

- **Forging your parents' signatures on progress reports, report cards, or notes from teachers. Even doing it on a field trip permission slip, because you forgot to bring it home on time, is cheating.**
- **Changing grades on tests or report cards.**
- **Writing a note to a teacher excusing yourself from something, and passing it off as a parent's note.**
- **Pretending you're sick and may die by sunset when you don't feel like going to school because of an assignment you didn't do or a test you didn't study for.**

I got caught for cheating on some tests. The teacher called my mother and we had a conference. I didn't have recess for two weeks. —Danny, age 11

USING THE INTERNET FOR RESEARCH

During the Dark Ages, when your parents were kids, card catalogs in libraries and encyclopedias were the way most kids found information for school projects. Now we also have the Internet, which makes doing research as much fun as watching TV—okay, *almost* as much fun. Sometimes this research device can be overwhelming or intimidating. Here are some tips on how to make the most of this amazing invention:

- Write down subjects related to your topic on index cards. Search some of them on the Web. You might find great information that will make your report or project seem absolutely spectacular.
- Don't feel dorky about using sites made for kids only. They usually contain information written in a lively manner. They explain things clearly and leave out useless details.
- If the words *more like this* or *find similar pages* come

up under topic headings, click to find out where these lead. You may find some sites or information that you can use.

- Click on words in bold. These may be links that lead you to more information about the topic. Before you click anything, write down the URL address of useful sites so you can go back to them if you get bumped off. If you like a site, make it a favorite.

- If a site offers an E-mail address or 800 number, write or call for more information—but make sure you get permission from your folks. Most sites are nothing more than they appear to be, but sometimes an innocent-looking site might be a ploy to get kids to buy things or set up inappropriate meetings.

- Take advantage of multiple search engines like Dogpile (www.dogpile.com). Once the engine comes up, type your topic into the search box and press Search. In this way, you can look through many search engines simultaneously.

- Sometimes your search may lead you to books on your topic via Amazon.com, the biggest Internet bookstore in the world. This is an ad for Amazon products. You don't need to buy the books, but you can use these suggestions to take books out of the library for research.

- Print any information that might be even remotely useful. Clip or staple multiple-page printouts together. Put what you found at each site in a separate folder. This way your Internet search won't turn into a mess of paper when you need to refer back to it—it's easy for that to happen.

INTERNET PREDATORS

It's fun to talk on-line in chat rooms to people whom you've never met. Sometimes you might even have talks with people you'd like to know face-to-face because you're curious, or it seems fun because it's risky. It's best to leave Internet friends as Internet friends only and follow these rules:

- Never give your real name, address, or phone number to somebody you've met on-line without getting your parents' permission.
- Never set up a meeting with somebody you've met on-line without your parents' permission. If you ever plan to meet, arrange to meet at a public place with your parent or an adult you know going along.
- Never tell anyone your password.
- If anybody ever threatens you, makes inappropriate comments, or uses foul language, let your parents know.
- Don't lead people you meet on-line to think you are older, wiser, or anyone other than who you really are.

SOME ADDITIONAL SEARCH-ENGINE SITES ARE

- Ask Jeeves, *www.askjeeves.com/*
- AltaVista, *www.altavista.com*
- Excite, *www.excite.com*
- HotBot, *www.hotbot.lycos.com*
- Google, *www.google.com*
- Lycos, *www.lycos.com*
- Yahoo, *www.yahoo.com*
- Refdesk, *www.refdesk.com/newsrch.html*

Before downloading any program, make sure you check with an adult in the house. Sometimes downloading can unleash a virus on your computer, possibly damaging its hard drive.

I love looking up things on the Internet. I can find some weird sites. Once, I found one on worms while fooling around and did my science project on worms and mud. —Jean, age 12

Internet information is often fun to look at and can offer entertaining facts. However, it may not always be 100 percent correct. Always verify it with in-depth sources from the library.

EXTRACURRICULAR ACTIVITIES

Besides being places to slave over academics, complain about lunches, and observe the soap operas of life, middle schools offer extracurricular activities. You don't have to join them. You don't receive grades for them or get paid to take part in them. However, participating is a great way to discover talents, explore personal interests, and make new friends.

Some activities, such as band, orchestra, student government, or science club, happen at school. Athletics, drama groups, or choirs might occur at a different location and could include students from other schools. Off-campus activities give you an opportunity to meet kids from other neighborhoods and offer the chance to compare schools, to brag or share horror stories about them.

The good news about extracurricular activities is that you're usually involved because you want to be—not because the school forces you to be there. However, they take time and commitment. They cut into your time for schoolwork, hanging out with friends, or vegging out in front of the tube. Even though you aren't graded on extracurricular activities, the group members and leaders expect you to show up regularly and participate without groaning about it. You may be required to find transportation and money for uniforms, dues, and, in some cases, outside lessons. So before joining an activity that requires more than just your warm body at a given time and place, check out all the details with your parents.

Here are some questions to ask yourself before signing up:

- Do I have the time? Don't forget to factor in time for any practice that needs to be done at home.
- Can my family afford any costs involved, or am I able to earn the needed cash?
- Am I joining because it's something that interests me, or because it's considered cool?
- Are there activities I would really love but am steering clear of because my friends think it's dork city?
- If the activity involves tryouts, do I know how to prepare myself? Will I be able to handle rejection if I don't make it?

I started junior high after going to a private school. I didn't know a single person. I joined the drama club and made lots of friends. —Rosemary, age 14

I always wanted to take tap-dancing lessons. My folks thought I wouldn't like it because it's not something guys usually do. Some of the guys I know made fun of it, too. But there's another guy in the class, so we're friends. The two of us and a couple of the girls in the class do things together afterward, like go to the movies on Saturday afternoons after class. One of the guys who made fun of it at first came to our recital. We danced to some cool music and wore hip-hop costumes, so he thought tap dancing looked like something awesome to do. —Andy, age 13

Sometimes kids feel pushed into activities because their parents want them to be on the team or to play a particular instrument. The kid would rather eat worms. If this rings a bell, you may need to talk to your folks. Don't start the conversation with, "I think playing the tuba sucks." Say something like, "I know how much you'd like me to be a tuba expert, but I'd really rather take tap-dancing lessons, play cricket, or learn to weave." Sometimes the only thing in your power is to be honest with your folks about why you dislike the activity. If your parents still expect you to participate in something that seems horrendous, grin and bear it. Maybe you'll like it better than you thought. And if it's horrible, at least your parents will know you gave it a chance.

Middle school means growing and changing. Sometimes it means trying to meet adults' expectations, even if you don't always want to.

4

PEERS

I know who my friends are . . . don't I?

If you're like most kids, people your own age are key to your existence. Some kids rate as best buddies. You can't live without them. You tell them your deepest, darkest secrets. They share theirs with you. They're as important to you as family members. Other kids may make your life miserable. You wish they'd move to Siberia.

In middle school, your behavior, interests, and friendship needs might change drastically. So might those of the kids you know. One day somebody is an incredible friend, but a few months or weeks later, you may wonder how or why you connected with that person at all. She may feel the same way about you, too, and give you not-so-nice clues about her feelings. In this chapter, you'll discover how to deal with friends and enemies without appearing clueless about socialization rituals.

FITTING IN

In middle school, being like everyone else, or at least like the kids whose acceptance you really want, becomes intensely important. Fitting in may mean wearing certain clothes or hairstyles or engaging in certain behaviors. Or it may involve *avoiding* certain clothes, hairstyles, or behaviors like the plague. Fitting in may mean changing yourself in major or minor ways so other kids will like you and be your friend. It's okay for your friends' opinions of you to be important, to some extent. But think hard before creating an entire new you to please other people. It's YOU that you really need to please—not other kids. If you're considering a total personal makeover, ask yourself these questions first:

- Is this what *I* really want, or am I doing it because it's who other kids want me to be?
- Do I absolutely need to act in a certain way to please other kids and earn their respect? Maybe they'll still be my friends if I don't change.
- If I'm making intensive changes to fit in, should I consider finding different friends?

I had a friend who kept telling me what to do, how to dress, and how to act, or she wouldn't be my friend. For a while I did what she said. Then I got sick of her and dumped her. I didn't want to be friends with somebody like that. —Judi, age 12

THE NAME-BRAND GAME

Maybe you don't care what you wear to school. Your mother buys all your clothes. In the morning, you pick up anything out of the drawer, closet, or off the floor and throw it over your body. But lots of middle school kids do care what covers their bodies. Sometimes this results in spending megabucks. You may feel you can't live without what everyone else wears. Sometimes your folks honestly can't afford to buy what everyone else has, or maybe they don't want to spend the money. Here are some techniques that, to some extent, might help you get by:

- *If your parents have budgeted for three new pairs of jeans for school, say, "I'd rather have two pairs," and have one of them be the more expensive kind. —Liz, age 14*

- *Baby-sit, mow lawns, offer to walk people's dogs. Use the extra money to help offset the price of the clothes. —Eric, age 13*

- *Go to a store that sells things for less. —Karen, age 12*

Sometimes you may not be able to afford the clothes, no matter what. Or your parents may not allow you to wear what your friends wear. In this case you will have to accept the situation, and so will the people you hang with. If they make remarks about your clothes or tease you because of how you dress, consider a serious friendship reassessment.

DRASTIC FRIENDSHIP CHANGES

You may have had a friend or friends in elementary school that you hung around with all the time. You ate lunch together and had sleepovers a lot. You shared everything. Maybe you bought identical outfits and pretended to be twins, triplets. Now you wonder if you really knew these people or why you ever considered them friends. Here are some reasons this could happen:

- Friends find a new identity that doesn't include the friends from the past. They don't want to be reminded of their old identity, so as they shed their former style and interests, they also shed their old friends.
- Friends become interested in the opposite sex. The other friends think this is gross, and they don't want to hear details about who's hot and who's not. Or the situation could be reversed.
- Friends find a new interest that they're unwilling or unable to share with their old friends.
- Friends join a clique that excludes other friends.

If you're the friend that got dumped, the scenario hurts. Maybe you can use some of these tactics:

- Try to make plans to get together. But be tuned in to reality. Your old friend may have new interests and less time for you.
- Consider exploring your friend's new interests.
- Discuss what has happened and see if you can still be friends. Communication is extremely important now. You may not be as close as you were before, but you will still have some version of the past relationship.
- If these suggestions don't help solve the problem, you'll need to let the friendship go. It feels crummy, but you can't force somebody to be friends with you.

I had a best friend who dumped me to be in a cooler crowd. It hurt. She even had a party and didn't invite me. When I asked her why, she said, "Everyone thinks you're a dork." I felt really awful for a while. But I found new friends and don't feel bad about it anymore. —Doreen, age 13

I was friends with a guy all through elementary, and we did everything together. Then he found a new best friend. We're still friends but not "best" any-more. That's okay. I've found two other close buddies. —Todd, age 12

If you're the friend who has drifted away, maybe you can remain buddies with your old soul mates, too. Here's how to handle this situation diplomatically:

- Introduce the old friend or friends to your new ones. See if they can connect. Clue your old friends in about your new interests. See if they'd like to share them with you.

- If a former buddy asks what's going on, be honest. Say something like, "I've found some new interests or people to hang with. I won't have as much time for you now, but we can still hang out sometimes." Don't say things like, "My new friends think you're a nerd" or "You suck at basketball, so stay out of my life."

  - *If you really don't want to remain friends, and the other person keeps getting in your face, just say nicely, "I just don't feel as close as I once did."—Rob, age 13*

Friendships don't always last forever, in middle school or any time in life. In middle school they may change constantly, so you'll need to learn to deal with it. Fortunately most middle schools offer lots of ways for kids to connect. Other good places to find friends are at religious or civic groups or community centers.

BULLIES

Wherever you live, wherever you go, there is a certain kind of kid everyone has trouble with—the bully. A bully is somebody whose goal is to make life miserable for his or her victims. Bullies threaten, tease, or physically attack kids. They have little respect for other people.

Some bullies don't act alone. They might control a small group of people. They encourage the group to treat a victim a certain way. The other kids might be afraid of the bully, or they might secretly (or not so secretly) enjoy sharing the bully's power.

Here are some bully avoidance tactics known to work. You may need to try a few different things before a bully totally disappears from your life. Bullies are a little like a bad case of the zits. They may not always vanish after the first attempt to zap them.

- Avoid the bully. This might mean taking a different route to school. You may need to enlist your folks or an older sibling to drive you.
- When the bully is around, walk away.
- Do your best to make sure you aren't alone when the bully is around. Steer clear of empty bathrooms, hallways, or stairwells that the bully frequents.

  - *I'd stay with my friends as much as possible if a bully was on my case. —Annie, age 12.*

- Don't hit, punch, or kick the bully. The bully may do the same to you. Fighting is *never* a good solution. Violence only creates more violence.

  - *I would ask the bully why he or she is bothering me and then tell them to stop it. Of course, I'd have a few other kids with me. —Alisa, age 12*

- Try to hang with a friend or two when the bully surfaces. Some bullies like to do their thing in private, so nobody knows that they're really a bully.

  - *I'd get my friends to confront the bully and tell them to cut it out, with me along, too. I don't think people like that want kids to get in their faces, so you'll kind of scare the bully away. —Nick, age 13*

The situation can get so out of hand that you may need serious outside help from an adult. Then it's okay to rat on the bully. Tell a teacher everyone admires and respects, and she may make the bully aware of his horrendous behavior and put a lid on it. Just make sure the bully doesn't find out that you told, or you'll have created a new reason for him to antagonize you. Sometimes there may be more than one bully, and you'll need to discuss all of them with an adult.

Sometimes bullies threaten to do horrible things like kill other people. They may possess weapons like knives and guns. If you are threatened with physical violence or see somebody threatened, you **MUST TELL AN ADULT IMMEDIATELY.**

A bully, or bullies, can make life so miserable for a victim that the person gets totally stressed out. The victim might consider retaliating by physically harming their tormentor or might react by harming him- or herself. If you, or anyone you know, feel this way or talk about this stuff, tell an adult immediately.

Don't ever be embarrassed to tell someone that a bully is on your case. Between 70 to 75 percent of all kids have been hassled by bullies by the time they reach eighth grade.*

*Weekly Reader, April 2001; Chicago Parent, September 1996.

CLIQUES

A clique is a closely knit group of kids who have some kind of similar interest. During middle school some kids form cliques or are invited to join them. Members have something in common. On one level, they're just friends that stick together. Maybe they like sports, music, or a certain kind of clothes—or making life miserable for other kids. Some aspects of cliques are super. They provide a sense of belonging to a group other than your family. They offer a source of friends for hanging out, doing homework, or gossiping on the phone.

Other things about cliques are not so great. They can be like exclusive clubs. In a very structured clique, one or a few people make up the clique's rules. Clique members get tossed if they don't follow these rules. The group may be very selective about who can join. Some cliques don't allow members to associate with people outside the clique and make outsiders feel like pond scum. This behavior might make the clique seem like the ultimate status symbol and have outsiders hot to get in.

If you're dying to join a certain clique, don't park yourself at their lunch table, or throw a party and hope the clique eagerly responds to your friendly overtures. Follow these guidelines instead:

- Think about why you want to be in the clique.
- Decide if it's worth following the clique's rules and possibly ditching other friends to be part of the group.
- Befriend one person in the clique. See what develops. That person may offer you an invitation into the clique. But the other members may not like the idea, so don't count on getting invited to their next major event.
- If you don't get into the clique, remain friends with the person that you hoped would get you in. Maybe one day an invitation will happen. If it doesn't, you've gained a new friend.
- If you do become a member of the clique, make an attempt to treat outsiders like human beings.

I was in a clique for a while. The girls decided not to be friends with anybody who lived in a townhouse, an apartment, or a small house. So I decided I didn't want to be friends with them. —Lila, age 13

I hung around with a bunch of guys who labeled everyone who wasn't good at school or in sports with nasty nicknames. One day we trashed a kid's locker who wasn't in our group because he made the honor roll. I felt really bad about it afterward and started to hang out with other kids. —Jimmy, age 12

The Popular Kids

At most schools there's a high-profile clique. Everyone knows who they are. The members of this clique have somehow come to be known as "the popular kids," "the cool kids," "the in crowd," or various other labels that denote that they're "better" than everyone else.

Some kids are so desperate to get into the popular clique they'd march naked at a school assembly to be accepted. At some schools the popular kids aren't admired only by kids, they even charm the teachers. They seem to run everything important—sports, cheerleading, and student government. So it becomes painfully important to many kids that they get in.

Think about

the popular crowd and the word *popular. Popular* means "well liked." Does that really describe all these kids? C'mon. Are the popular kids really liked by everyone—especially by the kids that they treat like dirt?

If you could rename this group, maybe you'd call it the power clique or the clique that many other kids look up to. (The clique that many kids suck up to would be more realistic.) What goes on with the popular crowd isn't different from what goes on in most kids' groups. The kids hang out, gossip, go places together. They worry about grades, zits, making points for the team, braces, and bad hair days, just like everybody else. They do spend some time deciding who should be asked into the clique, who to throw out, and who should be targets of nasty stares and remarks.

In case you're wondering what happens inside the top group, and who gets in, here's the scoop from kids who have been there.

WHAT GOES ON IN THE POPULAR CLIQUE

We do anything that goes on in a regular clique. We gossip more about people, I think. —Ashley, age 12

We have get-togethers and parties. The guest list to everything is always exclusive. —Jennie, age 13

We talk about the opposite sex a lot—like who likes who—and who's hot. —Ronnie, age 13

WHO GETS INTO THE POPULAR CLIQUE

To get into the popular crowd, you need to have hung out with certain kids since kindergarten. Sometimes, if you're lucky later, you'll make friends with one of the kids, and they'll get you in with the other kids. —Jessica, age 11

For girls, it's all about who the cool boys like. For guys, it's all about who the most awesome-looking girls like. —Ronnie, age 11

It's about clothes, money, and if you're good in athletics. —Jimmy, age 12

Lots of these kids' parents know each other, too. They're usually on the PTA and are room mothers. You really need to dress and look good to get in. We don't want to hang out with people who wear cheap or creepy-looking clothes. There isn't anybody fat or ugly in our group. —Heidi, age 12

Before trying to get in with these kids, consider if you really want to always hang around with people who think this way.

The way to feel and to be popular in the true sense of the word is to hang out with kids who think you're awesome and whom you feel the same about—people you respect and who respect you no matter what you like, how much cash you have, and what you wear. If you find it essential to be in the popular crowd, use the clique-joining techniques. Before trying them, think about what makes these kids different from everybody else, and decide if what they expect from clique members is really all that important to you.

Do they have lots of money? Do they all have a certain look? Do their parents all know each other?

If none of the traits that describe them pertain to you, or you're unable to achieve them, be realistic. You can try to get in, but if an initial attempt doesn't work, strongly consider cooling your efforts to be part of this group. Choose friends who will accept you for exactly who you are. Attempting to break into any exclusive group may make you the target of these kids' not-so-nice side. It could also turn off kids who are more appropriate buddy material.

THOUGHTS ON BEING IN THE TOP CLIQUE

I don't want to be cool. I'd just rather be who I am and do what I want.
—Gus, age 12

I don't want to be embarrassed by other kids who think they're cool.
—Alicia, age 11

I have a cousin who's in the top clique. She has to do whatever the other kids want her to do. I'd rather just be myself and not be part of it. —Sam, age 11

GANGS

Gangs are cliques carried to the extreme. They can be involved in illegal activities such as robbery and drug dealing. They can be involved in murder, too. Sometimes they entice members to join by offering them protection from outside violence or the chance to make money by doing illegal stuff. Gang members may coerce peo-

ple to join by threatening to harm them or their family members. If you're pressured by a gang to join, tell the authorities at school or notify the police—fast.

HAZING

Hazing means initiating somebody into a group with teasing or cruel jokes. In some cases hazing involves subjecting them to acts of physical harm or humiliation, like allowing members of the group to beat them up while everyone watches. Usually members of the group keep everything about hazing quiet. They don't want other people, especially adults, to know what's going on. They know deep down what they're doing is wrong.

Sometimes a group can haze somebody whom they have no intention of letting into the group. It's just done to be mean. Either way, hazing is a form of bullying.

If you're invited to be part of a group that involves hazing, think about it. Do you really want to be subjected to humiliation and physical abuse? Do you want to abuse and humiliate others in the future? Why are these kids acting so mean to their peers? Is the abuse so bad that you should report it?

Hazing creates a circle of violence. Most kids do it to others because it was done to them.

I was part of a group that expected you to shoplift something from a store to get in. One day somebody got caught, and his parents had to pay the store about $300.00. All the kids' parents got called, and we stopped doing that. —Jason, age 13

The Dump Report

Sometimes a clique—or group of friends—decides to dump somebody that's been hanging with them. They do horrible things, such as ignore their victim, humiliate him in front of people, make prank phone calls, spread rumors, and generally make his life a mess.

This is a form of bullying. If you are the person who is receiving the dump treatment, life is the pits. Here are some ways to handle the situation:

- Make new friends immediately, as in *now!* Maybe these people may not be considered as cool as your former friends. Who cares!

If the clique treated you this horribly, they weren't good friends to begin with, and it's best that they're considered history.

■ Talk to an adult at school whom everyone, even the tormentors, trusts, like the teacher that lots of kids corner to discuss the latest movies, sporting events, and hottest books. That person may diplomatically discuss with the group the inappropriateness of their behavior.

Here are other being-dumped techniques:

■ *I would try to find out why they turned against me and see if I could find a solution. If it didn't work, I'd find new friends. —Annie, age 13*

■ *Don't beg the group to let you back in. This is exactly what they want you to do, so they can gossip and giggle about it. I'd just find other friends or people to hang with. —Meggie, age 14*

PEER VICTIMIZATION

Sometimes not only one group acts nasty to somebody, but an entire classroom, grade, or school. An unfortunate kid is selected as the school outcast—or maybe two or three kids are getting the victimization treatment.

Lots of kids will do anything and everything to make the victim's lives miserable. They walk by the victim and say nasty stuff. They may even trash her belongings. Nobody will eat lunch with the victim, and people act as though she has a dreaded disease when she gets near them. Going to school becomes a horrible experience. Maybe you wish everybody would put a lid on it because you feel sorry for the victim. But you're also well aware that if you attempt to put the kibosh on the teasing, the next outcast could be you. Here are some tips for diffusing or stopping peer victimization:

- If you are a respected member of a group doing the tormenting, talk to some of the other members about stopping it. You may be surprised about how many people will follow your example and cut it out.
- If the harassing is done mostly by a clique, you may want to consider why you choose to remain friends with these people. Do you really want to hang with people who expect you to dislike kids and show them disrespect just because they do?

- You may want to talk to some adults at school and see how they can intervene.

    - *I would tell a teacher about how crummy that person is being treated. Maybe they could do something to stop it. —Kai, age 11*

    - *I would find out exactly what the person did to make everyone so nasty. Then I would talk to both the person and the group to see what could be done to stop it. —Annie, age 12*

If *you* **are a regular target of peer victimization, tell your parents or a respected adult. Maybe they can help you find ways to deal with the situation. Suggestions might include the following:**

- **Ignore the tormentors.**
- **Don't cry in front of the people who are harassing you.**
- **Find friends, so you won't be alone.**
- **Discover why this is happening, so you can find ways to change behavior that may be causing the ostracism.**

In extreme cases, changing schools may be the only solution. Find out if this alternative is available to you and your family.

In middle school, handling other kids includes dealing with yourself, too. You need to assess the situation before making a good decision. Respect yourself and the rights and feelings of other kids, too.

5

THE OPPOSITE SEX

We don't always see eye to eye.

In elementary school, the comings and goings of opposite-sex classmates probably didn't interest you too much. You realized these people came from the same planet you did. You may have hung out with some of them regularly and thought of them as friends.

In middle school your view of the opposite sex may change drastically. You're no longer deciding whether to consider them as friend material. You may think about them in terms of romance, which includes crushes, dating, and kissing. Or your feelings about the opposite sex may be indifferent. There is no official age when you're supposed to be ready for romance. However, this chapter will help you deal with situations that commonly occur when the opposite-sex scenario changes from strictly being pals.

CRUSHES

Sometimes you get strong romantic feelings about somebody. You like or love this person. Your mind constantly fills with thoughts about him (or her)—and you wish he'd feel that way, too.

The object of your devotion could be a teacher or other adult, a rock or movie star, or another kid. Crushes are normal. It's okay to daydream and fantasize about somebody.

In the case of rock and movie stars, it's cool to send fan letters. It's entertaining to plaster your room and notebook with celebrity photographs. Being a star means getting this kind of admiration. That's part of being famous. But it's not realistic to think you will ever have a relationship with a rock star. So don't save up your allowance for airfare to his hometown with plans to turn up on his doorstep and receive an invitation to dine in his fifteen-hundred-foot dining room.

Adults in your life, like teachers, counselors, Scout leaders, rabbis, priests, and ministers, may give the impression that they like you a lot. But this absolutely doesn't mean they want a romantic relationship with you. So don't send love letters or expensive gifts, make prank phone calls, or corner any of these people to confess your undying love. This will most likely embarrass you both. You also might feel ultraweird when the object of your affection acts clueless about what she interprets as strange and unexpected behavior.

In the case of a crush on somebody around your age, it's okay to make friendly overtures to see what develops, just as you'd try to encourage anyone to be friends with you. Maybe the crush could turn into a relationship and maybe not. Sometimes it's worth the risk. But if the object of your affection shows no interest, accept that the crush may not turn into the relationship you hoped for.

Sometimes you might have a crush on somebody of the same sex. It's normal to admire somebody—and in many cases wish you could be like that person or spend time with that person.

Crushes can be fun because you can daydream without ever having to deal with the emotions of a personal relationship. You definitely won't be subjected to any blowouts.

I had a big crush on a guy two years ahead of me. Actually, me and my best friend both did. We talked about what it would be like if we all got together. It never happened. But that's okay. —Aimee, age 13

I had a crush on my sixth-grade teacher. She was incredible looking. She was so nice. I kept going in for extra help in math just to be with her. I felt kind of funny when she invited the class to her wedding ceremony. I went and it was very nice, and I was happy for her. —Mateo, age 14

SHE LOVES ME—HE LOVES ME NOT

Once you're attracted to somebody, you may want to know if that person feels the same way. Sometimes she gives strong clues that she would like to connect—phones regularly, makes efforts to talk to you, or e-mails you, or suggests definite plans to get together. Or she may be too shy to offer clues.

  - *If you really want to be explicit, tell the person right to their face you think they're really cool. Then wait for their reaction. —Nina, age 14*

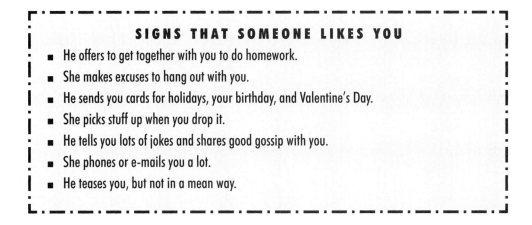

SIGNS THAT SOMEONE LIKES YOU

- He offers to get together with you to do homework.
- She makes excuses to hang out with you.
- He sends you cards for holidays, your birthday, and Valentine's Day.
- She picks stuff up when you drop it.
- He tells you lots of jokes and shares good gossip with you.
- She phones or e-mails you a lot.
- He teases you, but not in a mean way.

Somebody of the opposite sex may really like you. He may exhibit all of the somebody-likes-you signals and more, but this doesn't always mean he wants a romantic relationship with you. He might just want to be friends.

SIGNS THAT SOMEONE DOESN'T CARE IF YOU EXIST

- She ignores you.
- He doesn't return phone calls or E-mails.
- She turns down offers of getting together.
- He's polite to you, but never initiates a conversation.
- She teases you, but the teasing is mean, the kind that makes you feel rotten.

If you're going out with someone, it doesn't mean you're expected to spend every second with that person. It also doesn't mean you should ignore your other friends. Never drop plans with friends at the last minute because somebody of the opposite sex wants to go out. It shows a lack of respect for your buddies' time and gives strong hints that you don't value them.

If you find out somebody likes you, cool. Now you might be ready for the next step—going out.

GOING OUT AND HOOKING UP

In middle school "going out" can qualify as anything from sitting together at lunch to hanging out together at a group event, or actually going someplace alone. In many cases, going out involves asking a person of the opposite sex to do something with you. Or she may ask you. This can be mega scary. You don't know if she will answer with, "I'd love to attend the latest horror flick with you," or "I wouldn't be caught dead with you anywhere—ever!" Here's how to receive a yes.

- The best way to get a positive response is to ask someone who is likely to say yes. The girl in the other sixth grade that you've never talked to—or the hunky guy a year ahead who is going out with somebody else—are not the best prospects. They probably have not had enough interaction with you to start a relationship and will be clueless as to why you have a sudden urge to pair up.

■ Somebody that talks to you regularly, laughs at your jokes, and shares some of your interests may be thrilled that you requested to share quality time with them. Be specific. Don't say, "Would you like to go out?" without specifying a definite time or place to go. Here are some examples of how to ask somebody out, based on various personal situations:

➤ "Some of the kids are going to the school play this Saturday. Do you want to go together?"

➤ "Would you like to eat lunch with me today? My mother packed two walnut brownies and tuna sushi. I thought you'd like to share."

➤ "Do you want to get together after school today and walk our ferrets?"

If someone asks *you* out, and you want to go, answer yes, unless you need your parents' permission or aren't sure if you have plans. Then your answer should be something like, "I'm glad you asked, but I need to check it out with my parents, look in my assignment notebook, or check with my social secretary." Call or e-mail back as soon as you know one way or another.

Just say, "Want to hang out on a certain day?" Then make plans. —Willie, age 13

If you don't want to go out with the person, don't say, "I wouldn't be caught dead with you," pretend to throw up, or make faces. Politely say, "I already have plans, but thanks for asking." If the same person keeps asking you out, you may need to be more direct: "Gee, I think you're a great person, but I just don't see us going out together." Be as kind as you can, while still being clear about your feelings on the matter.

"**G**oing out" can also refer to an ongoing relationship. People have all kinds of names for this—such as hooked up, dating, going together, or going steady—depending on where you live.

If you play sports or perform in plays or musical events, it's nice to invite someone to come see you. Or you can cheer the other person on in whatever she is into. And it's perfectly okay to go out on one date with a person without forming an ongoing or exclusive relationship. If she hints or demands one, be honest if you're not ready for that kind of situation.

MONEY MATTERS

Be direct on how any get-together is going to be financed. If you're paying for tickets, all the Gummi Bears you can chew, and a ten-course meal at your town's five-star restaurant, let the other person know. If your date is expected to pay for his share of the event, be up front about it.

THE MYSTERIOUS PERSON DILEMMA

Sometimes you meet somebody you think is amazing! You received a strong impression that she—or he—found you awesome, too. You traded phone numbers and E-mail addresses. You try to contact her, but never receive a response. You're thinking that she dropped off the face of the Earth. You may even *see* her around. She either acts friendly or ignores you. You wonder what's up. Here are some ideas of what could have happened between that magical meeting and now:

- The other person isn't ready for a relationship.
- She is already in a relationship with somebody else.
- He connected with somebody else after he met you. He decided to spend time with that person instead.
- At the time you met, the person considered you amazing. Then his feelings cooled.
- She likes to collect the phone numbers and E-mail addresses of the opposite sex, without any intention of contacting the other person. Some people consider this a weird type of sexual conquest.

DANCES AND MIXERS

Depending on where you live, you may have the opportunity to go to events like dances, mixers, teen flings, get-togethers, or whatever your town calls them. Either way, you might be put in the position of asking somebody to dance with you or being asked yourself.

Asking somebody to dance is simple. You don't need to get down on your knees and beg. Just walk up, smile, and say, "Would you like to dance?" If he

agrees to saunter onto the dance floor with you, that's cool. If not, it's not the end of the world. Don't complain within earshot about what an enormous creep he is. Just ask somebody else.

If somebody who totally repels you asks you to dance, do not cringe. Just say, "No, thank you." If she continues to ask, say no, or dance with her once to help her self-esteem. Congratulate yourself on doing a good deed.

And just because somebody asks you to dance, that doesn't mean that you're attached to her for the entire afternoon, evening, and beyond. Dancing is just another way to relate to people and have fun.

I knew this guy from the school orchestra that I thought was cute. I asked him to dance with me at this dancing class my mom made me go to that I thought was for nerds. Now we're good friends, and we talk to each other a lot at school and e-mail each other. —Jane, age 12

Lots of guys are scared to ask girls to dance. So I go out of my way to ask them. I do it to stand out. Besides, I really like dancing with girls and talking to them. —Matt, age 13

It's kind of scary to ask a guy to dance. And it's a pain to stand there to wait to be asked to dance. I think dances are high stress. —Shari, age 11

THE PARTY SCENE

In elementary school boys usually invited other boys to parties. Girls invited other girls. Sometimes somebody threw a class party that included both sexes. Certain guests said "yuck" and wondered why the abominable creatures of the opposite sex showed up.

In middle school, party arrangements change. It's more common for both sexes to attend parties. The party may include danc-ing and kissing games like spin the bottle. People may hook up and do more involved kissing or personal contact, known as making out.

If you're comfortable with mouth-to-mouth contact, you may have a wonderful time at the party. Or you may feel so uncomfortable you'd like to crawl into a hole. Remember that kissing doesn't have to be on the lips. It can be on the cheek, hand, or arms. Here are suggestions for dealing with situations at kissing parties for those who want to participate—and those who don't.

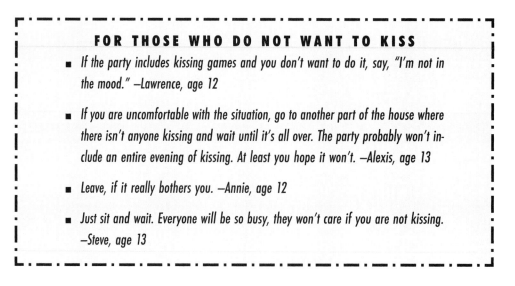

FOR THOSE WHO DO NOT WANT TO KISS

- If the party includes kissing games and you don't want to do it, say, "I'm not in the mood." —Lawrence, age 12

- If you are uncomfortable with the situation, go to another part of the house where there isn't anyone kissing and wait until it's all over. The party probably won't include an entire evening of kissing. At least you hope it won't. —Alexis, age 13

- Leave, if it really bothers you. —Annie, age 12

- Just sit and wait. Everyone will be so busy, they won't care if you are not kissing. —Steve, age 13

HOW TO KISS

Move your lips together slowly. Then part them. You can practice on a mirror, your teddy bear, doll, or pillow. If you're planning to kiss someone, always ask first if it's okay.

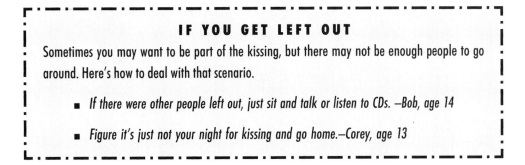

IF YOU GET LEFT OUT

Sometimes you may want to be part of the kissing, but there may not be enough people to go around. Here's how to deal with that scenario.

- *If there were other people left out, just sit and talk or listen to CDs. —Bob, age 14*

- *Figure it's just not your night for kissing and go home.—Corey, age 13*

Not everyone is interested in or ready for kissing at the same time. So you're not required to kiss somebody of the opposite sex to be considered hip—and you're not more grown up just because you're an experienced kisser.

THE OUT-OF-HAND SITUATION

Sometimes kissing leads to more than just kissing—and way more physical contact than you ever dreamed about. The other person may attempt to touch you in places you aren't happy about or try to remove your clothing. He or she may want to touch you where you wouldn't consider placing your own hands. You may try to pull away but could be ignored, and the hands may keep on moving. The person whines, begs, and demands for you to keep going, but you want to stop.

You should NEVER do something that makes you feel uncomfortable. Here are some methods to get out of a bad situation.

- Say no!
- If no is ignored, pull away and leave.

  - *If "no" and pulling away don't work, scream. —Megan age 13*

  - *I would call for help fast. —Annie, age 13*

If you are kissing or making out, the best place to do this is in a group—or a place with people nearby, in case somebody forces you to go too far. That way, the situation has less chance of getting out of control.

  - *I tell anyone, "This is a privilege, and we should stop when either one of us feels we want to."—Luis, age 12*

  - *I say, "We'll stop when the first one ready to stop wants to call it quits."—Ed, age 14*

If somebody doesn't want to go as far as you want, respect that. Don't force the issue. It may make her—or him—feel so uncomfortable that she'll decide not to be near you ever again. Maybe it seemed like she wanted to go as far as you did. People's minds can change as things progress. Everyone has the right to limit what they want to do with their body, no matter what the situation is.

SEX

When you're in middle school, people might refer to kissing, hugging, touching, or seeing unclothed parts of somebody else's body as having sex. These behaviors are really preparations for having sex and are called foreplay. These activities can be very exciting for both boys and girls. But don't consider them lightly. Sexual intercourse is a very serious physical and emotional experience between two mature people. You will learn a whole lot of truths and untruths about sex in the next few years.

SEXUAL INTERCOURSE

Kissing and touching can cause a boy and a girl to feel sexually aroused. The boy's penis may have an erection, and the girl's vagina may secrete a fluid, making it very moist. Boys and girls may experience an unusual sensation in their genitals.

These physical reactions are nature's way of making it easier for a male's penis to enter a female's vagina. Strictly speaking, this is sexual intercourse, resulting in the penis secreting semen, a fluid that contains millions of sperm. When a single sperm unites with an egg from the girl's ovaries, a baby may form.

There are many slang words for sex, including "doing somebody," "bong-ing," or "going all the way." There are many serious words for sex, too, like "making love" and "being intimate." People have sex for all kinds of reasons:

- To make babies.
- It feels good.
- Other kids did, or said that they did.
- They think the other person will like them better.
- They get a thrill out of making (and bragging about) sexual conquests.

It's wise to save sexual intercourse for when you're older and seriously committed to somebody and ready to take precautions against sexually transmitted diseases (STDs) and pregnancy. Many religious groups believe sex should occur only between married couples, and that its function is to create children. Having sex doesn't make you cooler or more popular or make other people like you any more than before. Sex can easily cause some-one to become pregnant or contract a sexually transmitted disease. Think about this: Would you be comfortable running into someone at school or at the mall if you had recently taken your clothing off in front of them?

CONTRACEPTIVES

There is no such thing as completely safe sex. However, a couple *must* use contraceptives if they wish to avoid pregnancy. Some contraceptives, such as condoms, also offer limited protection against STDs while others, such as birth control pills, do not. No contraceptive is 100 percent foolproof.

ORAL SEX

Oral sex means that somebody engages in mouth-to-genital contact on the other person's genitals. Some kids do it because you can't get pregnant from oral sex. Some kids do it because they think it's cool. Even though you can't get pregnant from oral sex, you can contract a sexually transmitted disease. Some STDs can kill you.

I like kissing, hugging, and a little touching, but I don't want any guy putting his hand inside my underwear, and I don't want to put my hands inside his. —Linda, age 13

My friend always brags and tells me what she did with guys and tells me I should do it, too. I'm not going to until I meet somebody special. —Alexis, age 12

I see lots of things on TV and in magazines about sex. And it turns me on. But I don't want to get stuck in a situation with some girl who gets pregnant or gives me a disease. So I'll wait until I'm really sure about who I'm with when I feel more ready. —Steve, age 13

A lot of guys talk about sex and who they'd like to have sex with. Some of these people aren't girls we even know. They're TV or movie stars or pictures from magazines. —David, age 12

Bragging, Lying, and Exaggerating

Sometimes you'll hear fascinating stories about how far so-and-so went with somebody—or several somebodies. You'll be amazed. You'll be dying to know all the gory details. What you discover could even change your view of the people involved. Whether or not the situation really occurred shouldn't alter your relationship with the participating parties. Their sex lives are their business. Whether Jessica let Elmer feel her bare breasts shouldn't be the basis of your continued or discontinued friendship unless they force you to join them—or you have an exclusive relationship with either one.

Kids brag about sexual exploits to sound important, or to make the other person involved seem like a victim of a sexual conquest. This shows a lack of respect for the privacy of the person or persons they've been with. The activities may not have even happened.

The situation gets stickier when the gossip includes you. Here's how to handle being the subject of sex-oriented gossip, whether or not you participated:

Talk to the people or person who is doing the gossiping. Tell them firmly you don't appreciate it. —Annie, age 12

If it isn't true, you may want to explain what happened to some kids. But just to people who you really care about. Telling everyone else looks dippy. —Nick, age 13

Stories about sexual exploits are part of middle school life. If you steer clear of situations that create gossip, however, most likely you won't be featured in these tales.

Sexual Messages Are Everywhere!

On TV, at the movies, in music videos, in advertisements, beautiful people seem to be always having sex or just about to. These people have amazing bodies and faces. In some cases they have incredible talent, too. You may think, If I had sex, I could be more like them. The messages don't really have

to do with enticing you or any viewers to have sex at all. They're about keeping you as a loyal fan, so that you'll continue to watch certain TV programs, movies, music videos, or so you'll buy certain products. What's going on has nothing to do with what *you* should be doing with your body. It's all about keeping you interested!

Be smart about what the imagery is telling you. Is it telling you that you must be beautiful or handsome to succeed in life?

That dressing or behaving a certain way will give you sex and make you happy? Middle school is a good time to begin to learn how to sort out media hype from reality and make up your own mind about what makes you and other people successful, admired, and happy.

I have to admit that I do spend my allowance on some of the neat-looking stuff I see on TV that awesome people use. It helps me feel good about being a little like them, even though I can't really be them. —Andi, age 13

When I see people doing sexy things on TV, I like to watch because I've never even kissed anybody before, and I want to know what it's like and how it's done. —Stan, age 13

Dressing Sexy

Because of the promotion of sex in society and the whims of fashion designers, kids can now buy extremely revealing clothes. They may want to look like models or dress like their favorite celebrities. They often show off lots of skin and body parts. The wearer may be subjected to annoying and lewd remarks by people.

Nobody has the right to say anything that makes you feel uncomfortable, no matter what you decide to put on or not put on your body. Ignore the remarks, and follow the same advice as if you were dealing with a bully. If the situation gets out of hand, tell an adult.

Unless your school has a dress code, you do have a right to dress however you want. Though you may consider rethinking your style of dress if you don't want to elicit suggestive remarks. You have to decide if wearing certain outfits is worth the consequences.

I like wearing what my favorite singers wear. It makes me feel good. —Cindy, age 12

In middle school, dealing with the opposite sex includes making lots of decisions. You need to think about what's right for *you* and what *you're* ready for. What everyone else is doing, or seems to be doing, may not always be the right thing for *you* at the moment.

6

HoME LiFe

If it's not my teachers or the other kids, then it's my family that's out to get me.

Families come in many forms. Yours may include two parents, one parent, stepparents, or a parent and his or her partner, as well as biological siblings, stepsiblings, cousins, grandparents, thirty-seven fish, ten pet snakes, or two dogs. Whoever or whatever makes up your family, you generally tolerated them in the past. You listened to them and sometimes admired them. You

played with your younger siblings when forced to. You didn't mind an opportunity to boss them around and beat them at board games. You looked up to your older brothers and sisters when they weren't acting like know-it-alls.

Now the entire family drives you bananas! You're not alone. Reactions to family members can cause major blowouts, where you slam the door to your room and don't want to open it again—ever. This chapter will help you co-exist peacefully with the people you live with as you journey through adolescence.

THE CARE AND FEEDING OF PARENTS

Long ago, your parents changed your diapers, fed you, and wiped your nose. When you came home in tears, you usually told one of them all about it. They tried to comfort you with words like, "Oscar was a big creep for not

letting you play soccer," or "Elvira should have invited you to her birthday party. I'm calling her mother."

For the most part, you could predict how they'd treat you in most situations. Now you're not quite so sure. One minute they tell you how grown up you are: "We're so proud of how you took care of your little sister Tootie when we went to Aunt Mahitabel's wedding." The next minute they won't allow you to do something everyone else can do: "No, you cannot walk to the corner drugstore alone after five P.M.!" Sometimes there's no telling how parents might react in a given situation.

The amazing truth is your parents are as perplexed about you as you are about them. They aren't always sure how to treat you in certain situations. You may act almost adult sometimes. Maybe you became a major part of the cleanup crew when unplanned guests decided to drop in with only ten minutes' notice, or you postponed a much-wanted trip to the mall to watch younger siblings when one of your folks had an emergency errand to run. But your parents may still need to remind you to flush the toilet, referee your food fights, and beg you to clean your room. You act like a kid on some occasions, and independent and grown-up on others. So your parents are learning new ways to react toward you.

Why Do They Need to Know So Much?

When you were a little kid, you eagerly shared your life with your folks. You wanted them to avidly listen to everything you said. Now you wish they'd butt out of your business. You can't stand their constant grilling about your comings and goings, in-depth questions about who you're hanging with. You don't need to reveal every detail about your life to your folks. Most parents don't require a list of who gets their period or who has had a wet dream, or an extensive description of the crumbs of food you left on your cafeteria tray. But parents do need to know about certain happenings. That's in the "parental bill of rights."

Your parents have the definite right to know about the following situations:

- Whom you're hanging out with. This includes your friends' names, their parents' names, and their addresses and phone numbers. Have your friends drop by so your folks can get to know them.
- Exactly where you are going, what you plan to do, and the times you will be doing it.
- How you are doing in school. If your grades are poor in a subject, your parents have the right to call the teacher and discuss it.
- How you are doing at the activities

they're paying for with their hard-earned cash, such as trombone, karate, and hip-hop lessons.

■ How you're feeling, physically, mentally, and emotionally. This means they also have the right to make you see the appropriate professional people if you're not feeling well.

Here's a big tip about handling parents. The more you share about what's going on, the less likely they will be to engage in annoying prying. So let them in on what's happening, and you might find that question bombardment eases up.

Parents Tell Us Why They Need to Know So Much

I want to make sure that everything is going okay. —Herb, age 52

I want to make sure my kid stays out of trouble. —Karen, age 47

He's a kid. So we need to know what's going on. —Clarence, age 48

Super Snoopers

Some parents are major nosy. They ransack their kids' bookbags. They read diaries and mail. They search the wastebasket for E-mail printouts or try to figure out ways to discover passwords. They're constantly on the prowl to uncover minute details of their kids' lives. Sometimes the snooping is out of curiosity, other times it's to discover what type of trouble the kid has been in or might soon be part of. Here are some ways to handle excess parental snooping:

- Tell them you feel uncomfortable about their detective work.

  - *Tell them you need your space. Ask them what it is they really need to know about. Then tell them. But don't tell them everything. —Jane, age 14*

- Discuss ways you can better communicate.

  - *Ask your parents about their lives. Tell them about yours. Tell them stuff you're sure they'd like to know. —Steve, age 13*

- Find out what issues they feel they'd like to know more about. Discuss how you can talk about them more openly.
- If you feel you need to be secretive about something, ask yourself why you don't want your parents to know about it.

You do have the right to establish boundaries with your parents. Discuss this with them, and then expect them to respect the boundaries you've agreed upon.

Ask your parents if you've done something to make them distrust you. But think this one over beforehand. They may feel they have good reason to prowl in certain cases:

- You forget to bring home progress reports from school, field trip forms, or notes from teachers.
- Your grades are poor. You're ditching school, lessons, or practices—or have had suspensions from school.
- You've been hanging with kids known to shoplift or experiment with drugs and/or alcohol or who are sexually active.
- You've are experimenting with drugs and/or alcohol, smoking, or shoplifting, or are sexually active.
- You have a new set of friends, and your behavior has changed negatively because of the association.

If this sounds like you, your parents have a definite reason to be concerned. If you want your parents off your back, consider engaging in more acceptable behavior. Then they might be less encouraged to pry. You may want to think about why you're involved in such behavior, see your school counselor to discuss it, and work on ways to change it.

If you haven't done anything to cause your parents concern, ask them nicely to stop snooping—or put the belongings they tend to rifle through in a special hiding place.

FREEDOM TO BE YOU

You're growing up and forming new ideas. You have strong desires to get out and into the world of malls, concerts, and hanging out with friends. You don't want your buddies to think less of you because you aren't allowed to do what they do. If your parents do not give you the same freedoms your friends have, this can create major hassles.

COMMON FREEDOM ISSUES

- Curfew
- Choice of clothes
- Makeup, tattoos, and piercings
  - Choice of friends
  - Places one is allowed to go
  - Dating
  - Academic expectations and homework
  - Outside lessons such as music, art, or dance
  - Chores
  - Room messiness
  - Phone use
  - Internet use
  - Allowance

Each family has certain rules and limitations about what kids can and cannot do. Some kids may be allowed to stay out all night, dye their hair pink, and get tattoos. Other kids have parents that monitor every second of television viewing and expect them to be in bed at eight-thirty on the dot. Parents don't set rules to torture their children. They set them because

- They want to protect you.
- You need structure in your life.
- They want structure in both your life and theirs, so that family dynamics will run smoothly.
- They have their own opinions about how kids your age should act and look. They've gotten some ideas about the best ways to raise children from their friends and relatives, how they were raised, religious beliefs, and parenting books. Now they're using what they know on you.

Pretend your parents don't set any rules, and you could live your wildest dream of doing whatever you want to do. You have no curfew, no academic expectations, and you can leave anything on your bedroom floor. Here's what could happen to you. You might stay out all night and worry your parents, if you had no particular time you needed to be home. You could get picked up by the police, if your town has curfew laws. If nobody expected you to clean up your room, you might not find the clothes you wanted to wear, or you might leave rotting food that attracted rats, mice, and bugs.

If you were given no expectations about schoolwork, maybe you'd ditch school, forget homework, and flunk. If you don't learn the skills that school can give you, you'll never get far in life and probably won't be happy.

Now here's a tip about parents: Not all parents are total ogres about what they'll allow you to do. Often they're hesitant to give you certain freedoms because they think that you aren't ready to handle them. So you need to prove them wrong. One way is to follow the *current* set of parental rules to the letter—and then some. It's a simple case of doing what *they* want so that they'll let you do what *you* want. The more you can show them that you are responsible and mature, the more you'll be able to negotiate rules in your favor. Here are some surefire methods to show the folks you deserve to do things they aren't wild about:

- Finish chores assigned to you without your parents having to nag you. Ask to do more.
- Act polite toward all family members, including siblings that are a pain.
- Bring home respectable report cards. Work on improving any grade they're not happy about. Chances are *you're* not thrilled about your low grade, either. Let your folks know that.
- Clean up any messes that you create—or that your friends make when they visit.
- When your parents are supposed to pick you up somewhere, be there at the agreed-upon hour. This way, thoughts about kidnapping and other fears won't run rampant through their minds.
- Don't whine, slam doors, swear, or threaten to run away when you don't get your own way.
- Point out specific examples regarding how much you've proved you've been able to handle responsibility.

■ *I talk it over with them. Sometimes we compromise. Maybe they'll let me do something like stay out later—but not as late as I really want. It's better than them making you come home at the time they wanted at first. —Arla, age 13*

It's best to negotiate one issue at a time. Don't make requests to pierce your navel, dye your hair purple, and join a group of hitchhikers to Guatemala all at once. They'll be sure to say no to everything and may refuse to listen to future requests.

Don't make requests when your parents or guardians are distracted or in a bad mood. Set up a specific time to discuss important topics.

"BUT EVERYONE ELSE DOES . . ."

Sometimes you're dying to do something everyone else is allowed to do. Maybe it's visiting the mall across town, taking bungee-jumping lessons, or getting tattoos. Your parents may say, "You must be kidding!" You feel like you're stuck with the most unreasonable, rotten parents in the world.

Be honest. Are *most* kids at your school really allowed to do the thing you'd like to do? If two buddies shave their heads and pierce their tongue, it doesn't mean that everyone else does. It means these two kids can look however they want. Your parents aren't being ogres by forbidding you.

Or maybe you *really* aren't allowed to do what *most* kids do. Maybe everyone attends sleepovers, dances, and parties, but your folks refuse to let you go. You may want to request that your folks discuss these activities with the other kids' parents or the adult in charge. Maybe they'll discover that what you want to do is common practice instead of being only for deviants.

I tell them to call the parents of kids that I know they like, to really check out what I want to do. This way they'll know that what I'm doing isn't just for troublemakers. —Marilyn, age 13

If the answer is still no, maybe it will be no for now—but not forever.

PHONE USE

When you reach middle school, the phone takes on new importance. It's your lifeline to the world. You need to gossip and make plans. However, you're also required to share this important instrument of communication with other family members who also have strong needs to gossip and make plans. This creates a dilemma when everyone wants to use the phone at the same time, and they all have the strange notion that their conversation is just as important as yours.

There are no set rules in the world for fair phone use. Everyone in your home may need to discuss agreeable time limits. This would include emergencies like the killer homework assignment that needs to be discussed in detail and crises with your friends that need to be averted and smoothed out. When deciding on fair phone usage, you need to agree on the following:

- Hours of use.
- Time allotment per phone call.
- What to do in phone emergencies, when it's really hard to end a call—or when you need to use the phone ASAP.
- How to respect everyone's need for the phone as well as yours. You may want to have a family meeting where everyone agrees to a list of phone rules that's posted by your home telephones.

Phone use costs money, and that might be part of the reason your parents may limit calls.

- *My parents set a rule for the phone—only fifteen minutes per call. —Stina, age 14*

- *My brother and I pay for a phone line by doing odd jobs like baby-sitting and mowing lawns. —Doreen, age 12*

You may want to suggest a second phone line. You can offer to pay for it from money you earn doing chores—or choose it as a birthday or holiday gift.

In some cases you may want to Instant Message or use E-mail instead of the phone. But you may also need to make agreements regarding on-line issues, too.

DIVORCE

Divorce unfortunately affects about half of the kids in the United States—so if your parents split up, you aren't alone. However, it stinks when your parents separate. Your parents are going through tough times. Think about how horrendous it is to break up with a close friend. Imagine if that friend had been your roommate and you'd had a serious commitment to each other and started a family. So if your parents act crabby, weepy, or moody, try to be understanding. Your parents still love you. Although they are responsible for the divorce, not you, their problems may affect you.

Once your parents are divorced, or even before, they might start dating. You may want to stuff the new person into a closet, tell them you hate them, or act like a horrendous brat so that they'll dump your parent. This is not the wise thing to do. It will only make that parent annoyed and hurt that you don't support his or her actions. Here are some general rules for kids when their parents divorce or are in the process of splitting up.

- Don't take sides or give detailed reports about every nasty word the other parent said or about their living arrangements, friends, or habits.
- If a parent is dating someone, act human when introduced to them and during the time you spend with that person. Don't tell them things like "I hate your guts" and "You're a rotten person."
- On the flip side, if you like your parent's date, don't give full-blown accounts of how amazing they are to the other parent.
- If your parent remarries, be civil to the new spouse. Same for the person's kids, even if you can't stand to be in the same room with them, because they have horrible habits like burping, drooling, or picking their nose.

My mom remarried. This included a stepsister my age who now shares my room. I guess she's okay for a stepsister. Sometimes I like her, and sometimes she's a pain in the butt. —Sharon, age 12

My parents got divorced. Then my mom moved away, and I don't see her that much. My dad met somebody I really liked, and it didn't work out. I was surprised I felt so bad when they broke up. —Jenna, age 11

My folks are divorced, and it's not so great all the time. I'm confused about which one I'd rather live with, even though I live with my mom. My dad lets me do things that my mom doesn't let me do. So I fight with my mom about treating me like a baby. My parents get on the phone and argue with each other—and I feel like I caused everything. —Bert, age 11

SIBLING WARS

Besides the grown-ups in your household, there are often brothers and sisters to deal with. Usually they are biological siblings. Others are stepsiblings that come into your family through a parent's remarriage. You've probably hated, loved, liked, and/or merely tolerated any of them at some point. Maybe you looked up to an older sibling who scared away bullies and threatened to pulverize them. You might have listened to their words of wisdom, like how to survive middle school and the rest of your life. Some of the advice you've probably used, but other words of "wisdom" you could have easily lived without.

Now you wish they'd all disappear. In this section, you'll get tips on how to deal with the other kids in your family without screaming at them or punching them.

The Bossy Sibling

Bossiness is usually found in older siblings. It has been known to happen with slightly younger ones, too. Your brother may think he is an expert on life, and constantly spouts tidbits of advice. In the past, you may have listened to everything he said, but now his advice, including on how to blow your nose, is driving you crazy. Here are some ways to deal with it:

- *Tell the sibling you appreciate his or her advice but you'd like to breathe, do schoolwork, or brush your teeth your way. —Annie, age 12*

- *Listen, but don't always take their advice. Sometimes a sibling doesn't really care if you do what they say. They just want to act like a know-it-all. —Ronnie, age 14*

The Tagalong

The tagalong syndrome usually happens with a younger sibling, but it can happen with a slightly older one, too. You have friends over. The sibling decides to join your group. You wish he or she would disappear or maybe never have been born. Or you're heading out of the house to go someplace when the brat appears and says, "Mommy said I could go with you," which may or may not be the entire truth.

You want to be with your friends without telling your little brother or sister, "Get lost" or "You're a grimy-handed little creep, and we don't want to be seen with you." Here's how to get the sibling out of your face nicely:

Tell the younger siblings that you'll do something with them later or tomorrow. Make sure not to renege on the deal. —Courtney, age 13

- *Occasionally allow the other sibling to do something with your friends.* —Lawrence, age 12

- *Offer special time to get together with them. Do something that they want to do, even if it's something you can't stand. But make sure you really do it with them. This isn't the time to make empty promises, because the sibling is sure to do something like report something you didn't want reported to your parents.* —Paul, age 13

- *I take my friends into my room. Then I lock the door, and we turn on the radio.* —Stina, age 13

If the situation gets out of hand, discuss it with your parents or have a family meeting. Explain that you need time for your friends without the sibling shadowing you.

Sibling Snoopiness

To many brothers and sisters, the comings and goings of their fellow siblings rate as highly entertaining. They may listen in to phone calls or other conversations, read notes, letters, or E-mail printouts, or go through bookbags or drawers. Information found may be shared with the adults in the house or, in some cases, the nosy sibling's friends. If this is happening:

- Check the other phone extensions when you make or receive phone calls to be absolutely sure the other sibling is not listening.
- If conversations are of a classified nature, consider conversing by E-mail. Throw out any printouts of the conversation or don't print out E-mails;

simply delete them after sending. (But keep in mind that this might not be possible with certain programs.)

■ Tell your sibling you don't appreciate their snoopiness. Get your parents to intervene if the behavior doesn't stop.

■ *Tell them how you feel about it. If that doesn't work, tell your folks. —Steve, age 13*

■ *Hide your stuff in a real good place. —Jennie, age 13*

You have a right to privacy from your brothers and sisters.

Sharing a Room

Sharing a room has its advantages and disadvantages. When everyone is getting along, it's like being at a sleepover. You can make gross jokes, throw pillows, and plot against your teachers and parents. When you're not getting along, it's like sleeping with the enemy.

When your body changes because of puberty, sharing a room can be embarrassing because you don't feel comfortable having another sibling seeing

you when you're not fully clothed. If there's a big age difference between you and the sibling or if the sibling is of the opposite sex, the situation can become almost mortifying. It's understandable you want your own room. Here are possible solutions:

- Some families may live in homes that contain lots of unused or rarely used spaces. These may be perfect places to park yourself. A rec room used for a once-a-year party or a den may be a perfect spot.

- An enclosed porch may be turned into a place for you and your stuff.
- You may want to consider always changing your clothes in the bathroom.

My younger sister and I have a room divider. She has her side. I have mine.
—Daniele, age 13

My mom gave me her sewing and craft room when my brother and I got too old
to share a room. —Carole, age 14

When I need another kid to talk to or feel scared after a scary movie, I'm glad to
have my younger brother around. —Ben, age 13

Your family may really bug you when you're in middle school. You're trying to become more independent of them and be your own self. You don't want to be exactly like family members or always follow the rules. But sometimes the choice isn't yours. Dealing with family during the middle school years and beyond means compromising, communicating, and respecting each other's differences.

Remember, your family is always there for you, no matter how often they drive you nuts. You just need to communicate and compromise, so your family dynamics can go as smoothly as possible.

7

PuBERTY

What's going on down there?

As if worrying about your friends, family, and school isn't enough, your glands are pouring out hormones and wreaking havoc on your body. It's definitely a different body than before. You're growing taller and wider. Girls sprout breasts. Boys' penises mature. Everyone develops more hair.

There's no exact timetable for all this, so if these things have or have not happened yet, it doesn't mean that there's something wrong with you. This chapter will give information about how to deal with major body changes and explain why they happen. There are many great books—such as *The Period Book* and *What's Going on Down There?*—that take an in-depth look at puberty.

HAIR, HAIR, AND MORE HAIR

During middle school, hair grows in places it never grew before. Everyone sprouts hair under their arms and in their pubic area, which is the area between your legs. Pubic hair is often darker and curlier than the hair on your head. Guys might find hair all over the place—on their shoulders, chest, legs, and stomach. Hair might appear on girls' legs or above their lips. Or hair that already exists becomes longer and darker.

In our culture females usually shave the hair under their arms and on their legs. So if you're a girl, you may want to remove your hair. That's cool. Boys may want to shave their faces. Getting rid of hair isn't difficult, but don't try anything without consulting an adult and having them show you how. Hair removal,

if you don't know what you're doing, can result in razor cuts or chemical burns from bleach or hair remover.

My dad showed me how to shave. I felt funny even discussing it with my mom. —Moss, age 14

There's one girl whose mother won't let her shave her legs. I feel bad because she really needs to, and some of the kids tease her about it. —Nona, age 13

BRACES

The need for braces seems to occur just when you start to care about your looks. Luckily, you'll only wear your braces for a short while. Braces are dental appliances that are attached to your teeth to straighten them so that you'll look, chew, and even talk better in the future.

Braces come with silver, clear, or even colored wires. Depending on your situation, there may be clear braces that fit over your teeth and are difficult to notice. Your orthodontist may even suggest lingual braces. You can't see these because they fit on the back of your teeth rather than the front. But they may take a little more getting used to because the bumpy parts are on the back of your teeth, and your tongue may hit them.

Wearing braces means you need to take extra care of your teeth. Food can become trapped in the braces, so you need to brush after every meal without fail. You might want to consider taking a toothbrush and toothpaste to school. And if you wear a retainer that needs to be removed when you eat, make sure you don't leave it on your lunch tray when you're done. It can easily take a trip down the cafeteria conveyor belt with your dirty dishes and then be crushed in your school's trash compactor.

I like orthodontist appointments. I schedule them with my best friend. Sometimes we get appointments during school hours and go to the Dollar Store and McDonald's before we head back. —Gina, age 13

ZIT WARS

You probably never gave your skin much thought until recently. But now you, or one of your friends, have been besieged by pimples. They can pop out anywhere, on your face, back, arms, or chest—wherever you don't want them to.

Here's why zits flare up: New hormones shoot through your body. The hormones cause your skin to produce more oil. The oil can clog pores, the tiny holes in your skin. If the pore becomes infected, a pimple happens. Here are some tips on preventing zits and getting rid of them. This doesn't mean you'll totally zap them, but at least you'll get them under control.

- Wash your face thoroughly every morning, afternoon (when you get home from school), and evening.
- Avoid hairstyles that touch a lot of your face. Your skin's contact with oily hair can aggravate pimples, so you need to keep your hair clean, too.
- Keep your hands clean and avoid the habit of rubbing your face.
- Try not to pop your pimples. If you can't resist, make sure your hands and the area around the pimple are clean. Put a warm washrag over the pimple before squeezing it. When you finish, wash the area again.
- Take advantage of over-the-counter creams or ointments available at your local drugstore. You might want to ask the pharmacist what to use for your particular situation.

- If all else fails, you may need to go to your family doctor or to a dermatologist (a doctor who specializes in skin problems). The doctor may give you oral medication that often makes the zits disappear. But you need to follow the directions exactly, or the pimples will return.

  - *My skin was kind of bad. Nothing helped. So my mom took me to the doctor, and I got some pills that made the pimples go away. —Jean, age 13*

PERSPIRATION PROBLEMS

During puberty, sweat glands as well as oil glands go into overdrive. Sweat smells, and stale sweat smells even worse. Many kids get concerned about B.O., or body odor. Taking a shower or bath daily is a good way to prevent B.O. So is using deodorant or antiperspirant. A deodorant helps get rid of the sweat's smell. Antiperspirants create a temporary seal that prevents perspiration for a few hours, and they control odor, too.

I wish everybody at school would wear deodorant—especially after gym. Some people really smell, and it's disgusting. —Diana, age 13

VOICE CHANGES

Boys' voices may become deeper in middle school. The vocal cords become longer and thicker. For some guys this happens gradually. Nobody notices until the guy's voice becomes deep. Other boys' voices change quickly. During the time a boy's voice changes, he can sound fine one minute and then high and squeaky the next. This can be very embarrassing. Fortunately it lasts only during puberty—not forever.

I was in my temple's children's choir. Then I had to drop out because my voice couldn't handle the high notes anymore. —George, age 14

GROWING BREASTS

For girls, one of the first signs of puberty is breasts. They develop anytime between ages eight and fifteen. Our culture makes a big deal about breasts, so they interest lots of people. This includes the girl to whom the breasts belong and the boys who notice the breasts.

When breasts begin to grow has nothing to do with how big a girl's breasts are going to be in the future. Breast size has nothing to do with how sexually experienced the girl is, whether she puts out, or how intelligent she is.

Growing breasts does mean that a girl will start wearing a bra. The best way to shop for a bra is for the girl to go with a woman she trusts, like a mom, aunt, older cousin, or sister. The adult of choice and the saleswoman at the store will help her choose a bra that fits. Once she's found the right size, she can decide about the fun stuff, like styles and colors.

Sometimes a girl hasn't grown breasts yet, and all her friends have. Some girls don't care about this. Others wear a training bra.

It seemed like everyone was growing breasts but me and showing off their bras when we got dressed for gym. So I wear a trainer bra. —Lindsey, age 13

I started to wear a bra the summer before fourth grade and needed it. I felt very funny about it. I knew that kids would stare at me sometimes and talk about it. But there wasn't much I could do about it. I just wish boys wouldn't stare at me because I'm bigger than any of the other girls. —Jan, age 13

PERIODS

A big change for middle school girls is getting their period. Menstruation occurs about once every twenty-eight days or so. Menstrual fluid, mostly blood, flows out of the girl's vagina. This can last for a day or two or for as long as a week. This is perfectly normal and no cause for a girl to be concerned. Over the course of the period, blood flow can amount to a few spoonfuls or as much as a cup. Periods don't usually hurt, but some girls may get abdominal cramps.

Girls wear sanitary pads or tampons to soak up the flow. A sanitary pad is an absorbent sheet of gauze-covered cotton that fits over the crotch of a girl's underpants. Tampons are tubes of cotton shaped like lipstick. Girls insert them into their vagina.

Periods happen because girls have two reproductive organs called ovaries. Every month one of the ovaries releases an egg. The egg can become a baby if a sperm from a mature penis fertilizes it. The egg travels to the girl's uterus, which contains blood-filled tissue that provides food and support for a fertilized egg. It's preparing for a fertilized egg to land and for a baby to grow. If the egg isn't fertilized, the lining dissolves. Then it comes out of the girl's body through the vagina. During the days this happens, the girl is menstruating, or "having her period."

No girl knows exactly when her first period is going to occur. If a girl has grown breasts and has pubic hair, it's likely that her period will happen soon. If you're a girl, here's how to be prepared:

- Even if you live with your mom and older sisters, it's good to have your own sanitary pads or tampons in a dresser drawer.
- Have your mom or an older sister show you how to put on the pad before your first period happens.
- Keep a sanitary pad in the bottom of a bookbag or in your purse. Periods come without warning. This way, you'll be prepared.
- If your parents are divorced, and you live with one parent and spend time at the other's house, it's a good idea to keep the necessary supplies at both houses.
- Girls living with a dad should let him know that she'll need to have supplies on hand. If it's too embarrassing, have a female adult discuss the matter with him. The situation may seem weird, but dads know about periods, too.
- Get a book on puberty and read more in-depth information about periods.

I am glad I kept a pad in the bottom of my purse. My first period happened at school. —Rosemary, age 14

I got my period at school, and it came through my skirt—not a lot but a little. So I wrapped my sweatshirt over my skirt so nobody could see the spot and went home. —Leah, age 12

BASIC PENIS STUFF

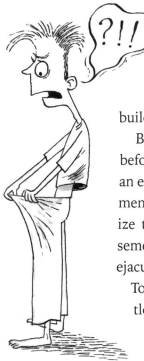

As a boy reaches middle school, his penis changes. It gets longer and wider than it was before. Penises come in a variety of widths and lengths. Size has nothing to do with a guy's body build, ethnic group, or masculinity.

Besides growing, penises react differently than they did before. Sometimes they get stiff and hard. This is called an erection. Sometimes a milky white substance called semen comes out. Semen contains the sperm that can fertilize the eggs that come from a girl's ovaries. When the semen comes out from a boy's erect penis, it is called an ejaculation.

To understand what's going on, you need to know a little bit about how penises work. A guy's penis becomes erect when the blood flow to it increases. The muscles at its base tighten temporarily, so the penis swells and sticks out. It becomes thicker and longer, too. This is perfectly normal. It's a basic human reflex that allows a man and a woman to have sexual intercourse and reproduce.

Sexual stimulation causes erections. And when guys are in middle school, sexual stimulation can be caused by lots of things, like looking at a girl's breasts, kissing a girl, thinking about one, or even talking to a girl. Sometimes erections happen for no reason at all. And it can be embarrassing. If you're a guy, and it happens a lot, you may want to wear loose pants. Sometimes you can tame your erection by sticking your hand in your pocket and pushing it down.

I got an erection once at dancing school when we were practicing a slow dance. I pulled away from the girl, and it went away a few minutes later. —Jon, age 13

Wet Dreams

Sometimes guys ejaculate while they're sleeping. When the guy wakes up, he finds a sticky white or clear substance on his bed. Wet dreams occur when a guy has a sexy dream or when the penis releases old sperm to make room for newly formed sperm. Wet dreams happen only while a guy's sleeping. They don't happen during class or while you saunter about the mall. But ejaculations can happen anytime a guy is doing something sexy, like kissing or hugging someone in a romantic way.

I had a wet dream. I threw my sheet in the laundry so nobody could see. —Ted, age 13

Athletic Supporters

An athletic supporter or jockstrap is something a guy wears during sports so that his penis and testicles won't bounce around and possibly get injured. It's an elastic belt with a pocket for his genitals. The pocket often has room to hold a plastic "cup" that adds extra protection. They come in sizes that correspond to the width of the boy's waist.

Athletic supporters can be purchased at a department store, variety store, or sporting goods shop.

I live with my mom—and never see my dad. I felt weird when I needed to get an athletic supporter for gym. I just gave my mom the list of supplies I needed, and she picked up everything and put it on my bed. —Allen, age 13

My family got really crazy when I got an athletic supporter. My mother took it out of the bag and put it on her head. Then I imitated her and put it on my head and started running around the house. The dog started barking because she didn't know what was going on. —Al, age 11

SHOWER ROOM BLUES

Middle school is usually the first place where in addition to changing for gym or swimming you and your same-sex classmates are forced to shower afterward. It can be awkward to be naked in front of people, especially ones that are practically strangers. That's for sure! To make things worse, during middle school, everyone is developing at their own rate. Maybe you're the one with an almost adult body, and you hope everyone won't stare at you in shock. Or maybe you haven't started developing yet, and you hope no one will stare. Maybe somebody in the shower room is making nasty remarks. The entire scenario makes you wish that the shower room drain would open wide and swallow you up.

You absolutely aren't the only one on the planet who hates gym showers. If somebody conducted an extensive survey, most kids would say *Eeew!* But many schools make kids take showers after gym because by middle school your sweat glands work in full gear. Gym causes you to sweat. Without a shower, you'd probably smell bad. If you'd rather eat worms than shower, here are some tactics to make it more bearable:

- *If you have some close friends in class, hang out together during shower time. But still take your shower quickly, so you can be out of there fast. —Sue, age 13*

- If somebody is making nasty remarks and it's really getting out of hand, tell your teacher or counselor. This is definitely a form of bullying or harassment and shouldn't be tolerated. Be discreet. You don't want the other kids to know that the whistle-blower is you.

A changing body is part of middle school life, just like any other issues. Learning to deal with it is part of growing up, and you'll have to deal with many challenges throughout life.

8

REALLY SERIOUS STUFF

Beware of the Dark Side.

in middle school you'll be exposed to situations that aren't easy to cope with. They may involve making tough decisions about things like experimenting with drugs, alcohol, or cigarettes or what to do about violence. Often you won't have created the situation, but you happen to get involved because people around you have made bad choices. Somehow their experience crosses your path, and you're stuck in a

situation where you have serious issues to deal with. This doesn't mean you'll need to move to another planet or hide under a rock until middle school ends. This chapter will help you handle some of the stickier and scarier situations that, unless you live in a perfect world, can arise in middle school and beyond.

TO SMOKE OR NOT TO SMOKE

It may look cool, grown-up, risky, and kind of fun. Your friends may do it in locked bathrooms, behind garages, or in vacant lots. Maybe your parents smoke, or someone famous you like lights up. Maybe you've heard that smoking helps you lose weight or reduce stress. Neither claim is true.

What is true is that it's addictive. It costs money, and it will eventually kill you. It also makes your breath smell. It makes your clothes and your hair smell, too. *Eww!* This doesn't mean you won't have friends that try it and who want you to join them. You may be teased or convinced you're a loser if you don't do it, too. It's very hard to avoid this kind of situation. Here are some things you can do:

- Be honest with your friends who are doing this and just say no thanks. Don't go into an in-depth lecture about smoking.

- If your friends tease you or make you feel left out, this could be a time to consider new friends. Not everyone in middle school smokes. Chances are that *most* kids don't.

■ *I say it will ruin my voice, and my voice teacher and choir director would kill me.*
—*Octavio, age 13*

■ *I just don't smoke. I don't need to give my friends any excuses. What they want to do is their business, and what I don't want to do is mine. —Anna, age 13*

■ *I say it will ruin my swimming ability. —Kevin, age 14*

DRUGS AND BOOZE

Kids involved with drugs and alcohol may also encourage you to share their experiences. It's not because they've learned in kindergarten that sharing is nice. It's because it gives them power to have somebody take the same risks that they took. Kids do alcohol and drugs, as well as smoke cigarettes, for various reasons:

■ They're curious.
■ They want to rebel.
■ They like the way it makes them feel.
■ They're bored.
■ They want to fit in.
■ Pop culture and advertising media make it seem glamorous.
■ It makes them feel grown-up.

You may be pressured into trying drugs or alcohol for any of the above reasons. The kids who do it may harass you if you refuse. If the entire group

you hang around with is involved in drugs or alcohol, and they use these regularly, you may need to consider finding new friends. If only a few people in the group are putting on the pressure, you may want to join up with the people who aren't doing drugs and try to get the others to stop. If this doesn't work, you and the others may want to dump the kids doing the drugs and alcohol.

Say, "I'm not interested." You may need to leave the situation fast. Sometimes it's very difficult to say no and really go through with not doing drugs or booze if all the other kids are doing it that time, too. —Rena, age 13

People just know I won't do it, so they don't ask. —Karen, age 13

PREGNANCY

Pregnancy is an unpleasant surprise to kids, to say the least. If it's you or the person you had sex with, you probably did not expect this to happen. Pregnancy happens because two people had sex and their birth control failed, or they didn't use birth control. This means that a baby is going to be born without adult parents to support it. There's a girl who will start to look pregnant as time goes on, and she's probably petrified to tell her parents. If you're the girl, you need to tell your parents—no matter what. If you're the guy, and the girl decides to have the baby, you may be responsible for the child's financial support once you turn eighteen.

Since the girl carries the baby, she or her parents make the decision, legally speaking, depending on what state you reside in. There are several options:

- The girl can keep the baby. She and her family will care for it. The boy could be involved from the start and possibly share in raising the child, too. When he becomes an adult he'll also permanently share in the financial obligations. The parents of the child may eventually get married.
- Once the baby is born, it can be given up for adoption.
- The girl can have an abortion, ending the pregnancy. The only place this should be done is in a doctor's office with the girl's parents' consent. Drinking substances, tak-

ing certain types of baths, or heavy exercise will not make a girl miscarry. Any attempt to abort a pregnancy that does not involve a doctor can be dangerous to the girl's health or even fatal.

Abortion is the removal of the baby from the female's body before the baby is born. It causes the baby to die. Abortion is not a method of birth control. It is an option that must be thought over carefully before it is decided on, and in most states girls under a certain age are legally required to have their parents involved in the decision-making process. No matter what your stance on abortion is—religious, political, or otherwise—it is a decision that you should want to avoid having to make at all costs. And the only way to do that is to avoid getting pregnant.

If you are pregnant or have gotten somebody pregnant, you must tell an adult. This is not the time to rely on advice from friends who convince you that they're in the know.

Getting pregnant can keep you from having fun. Once you have the baby, you have to take care of it. —Aimee, age 14

Getting pregnant probably changes everything about somebody's life, no matter whether the girl keeps the baby, gives it up, or has an abortion. —Lenny, age 15

I planned to go to college on a scholarship, but my girlfriend got pregnant. So now I'm working at a hamburger place to support the baby. My plans are on hold. —Jon, age 17

I have a baby. His diapers need to be changed. He needs to be fed. I love him but I can't do what I want anymore. —Kara, age 15

No matter how somebody deals with the pregnancy, it's a traumatic and life-altering event that every teenager should definitely avoid. Here are some Web sites that might help you decide what to do if you or your partner becomes pregnant:

- *www.teenwire.com* This site is sponsored by Planned Parenthood of America. The organization can also can be contacted at 1-800-230-PLAN. They will give you the phone number to the center nearest you where you can talk to counselors who will help you decide what to do.
- *www.teenpregnancy.org* This site is for teens and their parents. It contains interviews with teenagers who have become pregnant and offers tips for preventing pregnancy.
- *www.teenshelp.faithweb.com/pregnancy.html* This site offers many options concerning teen pregnancy and links to information about other issues.

VIOLENCE

It's horrendous when the place you go to school isn't safe. It's upsetting when you're threatened to give up lunch money or possessions even once, much less on a regular basis. Nobody wants to think about being attacked while walking through the hallway or heading in and out of the bathroom stalls. It's scary to show up daily at a place where kids get beaten up and students carry weapons. You can't totally stop violence in the world, but you can make some attempts to steer clear of it. Here's how:

- If it's common knowledge that incidents happen at certain locations, avoid them. If it's in hallways or bathrooms, visit these places with friends—never alone.
- Stay away from kids known to cause violence. If they try to befriend you, politely blow them off. If they persist, let an adult know about it.
- If you hear rumors that violence might be erupting, warn the principal or another adult.
- When you see any violence occur, don't stop to gawk! The people involved in the violence could turn on you. Leave the area immediately. Then report it.

Here's the address of the National Campaign Against Youth Violence, a Web site that offers tips about preventing violence in your community: *www.noviolence.org.*

I go to a school that seems safe, but there are kids who start fights and steal. The only thing I can do is stay away from these kids.

Sometimes it's difficult. Once I got my calculator stolen. Now I really watch my stuff. —Edgar, age 13

There was a kid who brought a knife to school. I got scared, so I told the teacher. She reported him to the principal. He got suspended for two weeks. —Miguel, age 12

SEXUAL HARASSMENT

In middle school, you may be exposed to unwanted sexual remarks, actions, or advances. You wish that the person making them would disappear from the face of the Earth. If that's happened, you are being sexually harassed. Or maybe you're engaging in behavior that totally embarrasses someone of the opposite sex. In this instance you might be the one harassing people. In case you aren't sure, here are some examples of sexual harassment:

- Leers or stares that make a person feel as though you're undressing them in public.
- Motions or sounds that pantomime kissing or any other sexual act and are intended to make a person feel uncomfortable.
- Unwanted touching.
- Making remarks or writing notes about sexual acts someone would like to do.
- Making audible remarks about people's body parts.
- Bra snapping.
- Asking sexually oriented questions.

- Discussing sexual topics when the other person seems repelled.
- Pressuring somebody to kiss, make out, or do anything else involving physical contact.

If you are a victim of sexual harassment in or out of school, tell an adult. If sexual harassment is happening at school, it's not only highly unacceptable behavior, it's also against the law.

If you're engaging in any behavior that's considered sexual harassment, make these actions history. Harassment makes the victim feel powerless. If you're sexually harassing people, you should talk with your school counselor.

There was a dentist who put his hands on my chest when I saw him for appointments. So I told my mother. She called the Better Business Bureau and the Dental Association. —Jean, age 13.

There are some guys at school that were saying all kinds of sex-talk things to girls. They were even grabbing us on the playground and snapping our bras. So my friends and I told our parents. Then we had a meeting with the principal, the guys, their parents, and our parents. The guys cut it out after that. —June, age 13

A girl at school kept following me and telling me how cute I was. Then she wrote me letters telling me what a stud I was and wanted to see my you-know-what. I told her I was not interested. She didn't get it at first, until I told her I'd tell every guy I knew about her stalking me.—Jon, age 12

You may wonder how flirting differs from sexual harassment. Flirting is done to show how much you like somebody and to get them to like you. Sexual harassment is done to tease somebody and/or make them feel uncomfortable. Keep in mind that sexual messages can be easily misconstrued. What might be flirting to you may be harassment to someone else, and vice versa.

SEXUAL ABUSE

Sexual abuse goes further than sexual harassment. It means touching, fondling, or actually having sex with someone against their will. Forcing sex on someone is an illegal act known as rape. Sexual abuse is usually perpetrated by someone the victim knows, such as a teacher, relative, or friend. If this happens to you, remember that it's not your fault. You want the abuse to stop immediately and have the person who's doing it punished appropriately. So you'll need to tell a trusted teacher, minister, rabbi, or other adult—or even a police officer. If you're not sure if a situation is abuse or if you otherwise need help, call or e-mail the Rape, Abuse & Incest National Network at 1-800-656-HOPE (4673), www.rainn.org, or Child Help USA at 1-800-4-A-Child (1-800-422-4453), www.childhelpusa.org.

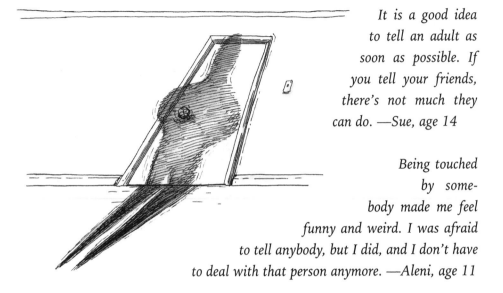

It is a good idea to tell an adult as soon as possible. If you tell your friends, there's not much they can do. —Sue, age 14

Being touched by some-body made me feel funny and weird. I was afraid to tell anybody, but I did, and I don't have to deal with that person anymore. —Aleni, age 11

Tell an adult no matter how dirty it makes you feel. —Vicki, age 15

DATING VIOLENCE

Sometimes you may be in a relationship that is difficult. A person you are seeing makes physical assaults, threatens you, or yells at you. They constantly say things that make you feel bad about yourself and make you question your self-worth. The abuse is not your fault. It's the other person's problem. If this is occurring, you may need to speak to a trusted adult who will help you deal with the situation. You may find out that it is time to end what may be an abusive relationship.

If something doesn't feel right, it probably isn't. —Lisa, age 13

He had brainwashed me into thinking it was my fault. —Steph, age 15

Get out before it's too late and you really get hurt. —Amber, age t/k

Abuse isn't just hitting. It means somebody constantly yelling at you and telling you they wish you weren't born. —John, age 15

If you feel you are in an abusive relationship, here is the Web site and telephone number of an organization that might be able to help: www.bradley angle.org/For_Teens/teen_dating_violence.htm. The Bradley-Angle house can be reached by telephone at 1-503-281-2442. You may call them collect.

DOMESTIC VIOLENCE

Sometimes life at home is difficult. You or others in your family are victims of physical assault or regular threats of attacks. Or maybe family members are yelled at and criticized so often that their feelings of self-worth are very low. If you feel this is happening in your family, you may want to talk to a

trusted adult, such as a school counselor. They will begin to help you view the situation more clearly and give you advice on how to deal with it. You may want to look under "Crisis Intervention Services" in the Yellow Pages or try calling or e-mailing the Covenant House Nine Line at 1-800-999-9999, www.covenanthouse.org, or the Girls and Boys Town National Hot Line at 1-800-448-3000, www.girlsandboystown.org. Or you may want to call some of the phone numbers listed in the previous section.

Middle school sometimes means dealing with troubling situations of a kind you never expected or experienced. If you've thought the scenario over carefully, you'll be able to make choices you feel good about when these situations come up.

Sometimes a situation may seem so hopeless that you may consider running away from home. Don't do it! It will not solve your problems. Many runaways return home. Some become involved in drugs, prostitution, or more abusive situations. In some cases, runaways have been killed. If you are considering running away, consult a trusted adult or call one of the phone numbers in the phone book. Counselors will give you advice on how to handle your situation.

9
Being Yourself

After all, that's who I really am.

In middle school you're growing in every aspect—physically, emotionally, and mentally. You're changing from a child into a teenager, which is almost an adult. You're learning how to cope with the new you. You're constantly bombarded with cues about what a middle school kid should be like. Some of these messages affect your self-esteem. Self-esteem is how you view yourself. Some people have high self-esteem. Other people have low self-esteem. Most people fall somewhere in between, and from day to day your self-esteem may change.

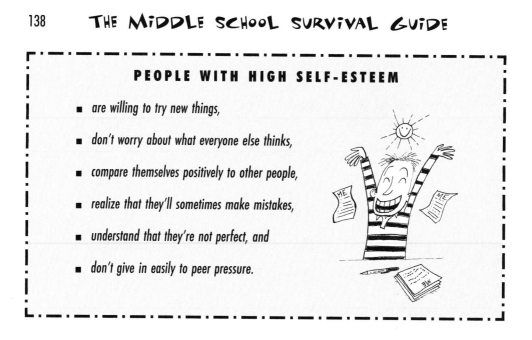

PEOPLE WITH HIGH SELF-ESTEEM

- are willing to try new things,

- don't worry about what everyone else thinks,

- compare themselves positively to other people,

- realize that they'll sometimes make mistakes,

- understand that they're not perfect, and

- don't give in easily to peer pressure.

The world's expectations about what middle school kids are supposed to be like can seriously affect your self-esteem. When you meet these expectations, your self-esteem rises, but when you don't, your self-esteem plunges. Most kids don't fit the complete image. Few kids wear all the "right" clothes, have stellar looks *and* awesome grades, *and* excel at every extracurricular activity.

If you can't behave in ways to please your friends or meet media-generated standards, think it over. Is what's expected really important to you? If adults in your life have expectations you can't meet, talk this over with them. Maybe you can modify their hopes. It's normal for self-esteem to change from day to day and in certain situations.

PEOPLE WITH LOW SELF-ESTEEM

- *are afraid to try new experiences because they fear that they may look foolish if they fail,*

- *worry about what everyone else thinks because they are unable to rely on their own opinion of themselves,*

- *compare themselves negatively to other people,*

- *have difficulty recovering when they make mistakes,*

- *think they need to be perfect, and*

- *give in easily to peer pressure because they are afraid to stand up for themselves.*

Some days your self-esteem may be high, and on others it may be low. Here are some ways you can develop your self-esteem:

- Follow through on what's expected of you at home and at school. It definitely doesn't heighten your self-esteem when everyone's nagging you to get things done.

- Tell yourself you've done a good job when you've accomplished something that means a lot to you.

- Make good choices. Think over your actions before you do anything you consider questionable.

- Try something new. You may or may not be terrific at it, but at least you've broadened your experience.
- Compile a list of your skills and talents. Include everything that you're good at.
- Create a list of things that make you feel good about yourself. They can be things that don't have to do with school or skills. Here are some examples:
  - I know a lot about black-and-white movies. It's fun to watch them with my stepdad and my mom.
  - I don't mind playing with my little sister. Actually, it's kind of fun.
  - I'm responsible for Rocky, my dog, and take good care of him, as well as my six pet rats and two tanks of tropical fish.

People with good self-esteem set realistic goals, ones that they can reach. Start a goal journal. Write down some objectives you'd like to reach, and give each one a time limit. Choose a goal you'd like to reach in a week, another you'd like to reach in a month, and one you'd like to reach in a year. Visualize yourself reaching your goals.

When you succeed, say "Good job" to yourself, and reward yourself. Eat a special treat, or go for a swim, do some hip-hop dancing to your favorite music, or read a juicy novel. If you don't reach a goal, think about why. Maybe the goal was unrealistic and needs rethinking and/or revision.

By developing your self-esteem, you'll make yourself more self-reliant, form your own independent point of view, stand up for what you think is right, and try your hardest in all that you do.

Here are some words of wisdom from other kids who have been through middle school. Think about their ideas, and use them if you wish. Then write down some of your thoughts about middle school. Jot down some thoughts about how you feel when you first begin, then write down your feelings after you've been there a while. Compare your feelings and see how they may have changed or remained the same.

Don't act too old for your age and don't think you know everything, because you don't. —Sarah, age 14

Be yourself. —Brian, age 13

Be nice to everyone. You never know if somebody who you thought was a nerd could turn out to be not so nerdy and an awesome friend. —Chaim, age 14

Create close bonds with other students. —Heidi, age 13

Work hard and get good grades. —Greg, age 12

Stay focused on your work at school. If you get behind, it can really be horren-dous. —Jimmy, age 12

Don't get into the superficial self-absorbed popular clique. It doesn't mean a thing. —Heidi, age 14

Don't let anybody pressure you into something that you don't want to do. Stand up for what you believe in. —Dina, age 12

Don't follow your friends just to be cool. —Tanya, age 14

As you continue through middle school, you'll think of quotes of your own. Write them down in a special notebook and date them. Read them from time to time to see how you and your ideas change throughout the next few years.

Middle school is a time to work on yourself and to learn to think for yourself. It's a time to figure out who you are. It's okay for your ideas and opinions to change throughout the next few years. They will be changing throughout middle school and throughout life. Good luck in middle school and in coming closer to the person you'd like to be!

iNDEX

Page numbers in italics indicate text in boldface and in boxed text.

Arlene Erlbach is the author of more than forty-five books for kids, including *Real Kids Taking the Right Risks: Plus How You Can, Too!; The Kids' Invention Book; The Kids' Business Book;* and *The Kids' Volunteering Book*. She lives in Morton Grove, Illinois.

Helen Flook is the illustrator of *The Town That Floated Away* by Sandra Birdsell, as well as the Max-A-Million Series by Trina Wiebe: *Max the Mighty Superhero, Max the Movie Director,* and *Max the Magnificent*. She lives in Guelph, Ontario, Canada.

OTHER BOOKS BY WALKER & COMPANY

The Period Book: Everything You Don't Want to Ask (But Need to Know)
by Karen Gravelle & Jennifer Gravelle

What's Going on Down There? Answers to Questions Boys Find Hard to Ask
by Karen Gravelle, with Chava and Nick Castro

Girl Talk: Staying Strong, Feeling Good, Sticking Together
by Judith Harlan

Girl Thoughts: A Girl's Own Incredible, Powerful, and Absolutely Private Journal
by Judith Harlan

5 Ways to Know About You
by Karen Gravelle

The Boy's Book of Lists
by David P. Langston

The Best Friends' Handbook: The Totally Cool
One-of-a-Kind Book About You and Your Best Friend
by Erica Orloff and Alexa Milo